*If This Is A Secret
Why Am I Telling It?*

ALSO BY RUSSELL L DRAKE

A Walk in the Park
The Sounds of Truth

Spoken Word Jazz CD
When I Think of You

If This Is A Secret Why Am I Telling It?

Thirty-One Secrets to
Living Life with Passion and Purpose

Russell L Drake

Order this book online at www.trafford.com
or email orders@trafford.com

Most Trafford titles are also available at major online book retailers.

Print information available on the last page.

ISBN: 978-1-4269-1938-1 (sc)
ISBN: 978-1-4269-1939-8 (hc)

Library of Congress Control Number: 2009939379

Trafford rev. 06/22/2018

 www.trafford.com

North America & international
toll-free: 1 888 232 4444 (USA & Canada)
fax: 812 355 4082

For Qierra, Sasha, BJ and Devin

Contents

If This Is A Secret
Why Am I Telling It?

Prologue

Quiet set over the room as the shadows of the evening crept upon the library walls. I lit the kindling in the fireplace to ward off the coolness in the air. My library study has always been a place of peace and solitude. The books that line the walls are precious to me. The answers to any question I had ever asked were in them. I feel at ease knowing their reference is available to me when needed. I hear a soft knock at my door.

"Come in," I call out. My son enters the room. He takes after me tall and easygoing. He also enjoys the solitude and peacefulness of the room.

"Dad?"

"Yes, Son, what can I do for you?" He walks to the front of my desk and sits down in one of the chairs.

"Dad, it's time we had that talk."

I raise an eyebrow. "Didn't we have that talk when you were ten?"

"Not that talk Dad. I mean the one about how you have made it in life. I want to know your secret to making it."

I ease back in my chair and looked my son squarely in the eye. "What do you think the secret is?"

He hesitates and looks down at his shoes. He knows when I answer a question with a question he is supposed to know the answer already.

"I don't know for sure but money has something to do with it."

I look at my son but did not say anything.

"Well maybe not just money Dad. You have always told me to put everything I had into whatever I do. I should care about it and stick to it."

I just sit there looking at my son. He starts to feel a little uneasy because he has not thought his question through before he asked it. I have always taught him to do that and he wishes he had remembered before he walked in.

"What else Son?" I asked.

"I should have a reason for doing what I do."

I smiled at him. "There you have it. You have described passion and purpose. That's my secret which is no secret at all. If it were a secret, I would not tell it. I live life with passion and purpose."

"What about money, Dad?"

"Money will take care of itself when you are passionate about life and have a purpose."

"So how do I do it? I hear the words but I am looking for something a little more concrete not as abstract."

"That's a good question." I reach into my desk and pull out a folder and hand it to him. "This is a manuscript that I am preparing for publication. Read it and we will discuss what you think of it."

He opens the folder and scanned the headings of the chapters.

I watch him as he reads over the topics of the manuscript and speak when he glances up.

"Son, the combination of the thirty-one lessons in your hand supports my philosophy for living life with passion and purpose. The current order is for my benefit and how I remember them. Every element can stand alone. The only exception is the first one. You must start there."

1

Love Who You Are

Love yourself. You are unique. You are one of a kind. Your life is fullest when you are able to help others. Here's the catch. You need to love yourself to effectively help others.

A mother fox had a large litter during the winter. Every day she would venture into the woods to find food. Day by day she fed her litter but neglected herself. Undernourished the mother fox died leaving the litter unprepared to fend for themselves. They perished too.

The mother fox hunted for her litter and did so unselfishly. She did not however take care of herself and sacrificed the survival of her litter.

Flight attendants instruct parents to put their oxygen mask on first when it drops and then assist their child. Why? To be sure the parent will be able to assist their child. If the parent blacks out who helps the child?

Are you starting to get my drift? Loving who you are is like the foundation of a house. In order to build a sturdy house you must have a solid foundation.

Believe in yourself. You must be confident in who you are and how you act. Believe that you are a person capable of receiving and giving love.

We get in our own way. We listen to others rather than believe in ourselves. There are people who are uneasy with the idea of loving who you are. They characterize this approach as selfish. Selfish is being concerned chiefly or only with oneself, without regard for the well-being of others. You are not selfish when you love who you are because you have a higher purpose that includes others.

Trust your instincts. Sometimes you just know. You may not be able to explain it. You have this deep feeling within yourself. Go with it. If you were given information from someone you love and trust what would you do? Chances are you would accept the information and act on it accordingly. Why not do the same thing with yourself? Trust your instincts.

Make time for yourself. I know what you are saying? Here he goes again. Me. Me. Me. Yes, you are correct but this is about recharging and refreshing you.

My laptop has a rechargeable battery. It will give me good service for a limited time. However, after a certain period, I will get a warning to plug in the charger or else I could lose all my work. Did I just compare you to a laptop? Yes I did. You have to recharge and refresh in order to do what you need to do. For you that may mean a good night rest, reading a book or any number of activities that help you recoup your strength.

"Master, which is the great commandment in the law? Jesus said unto him, Thou shalt love the Lord thy God with all they heart, and with all they soul, and with all they mind. This is the first and great commandment. And the second is like unto it, Thou shalt love thy neighbor as thyself."

(Matthew 22:36-39)

So in order to love your neighbor, you must love yourself. Your own love is the foundation that supports your love for your family and others. Love who you are.

2

Invest in Your future

Investments come in many forms. You should invest in education, your financial health and your community.

Investing in education is a lifelong endeavor. Education transforms us. In early America, slaves were forbidden to learn how to read or write. Why? Knowledge fed dissatisfaction and spawned unrest against the unjust system that held them.

Education can change ones circumstances no matter who you are. The desire to learn will help you become whatever you want to be.

Our state educational systems are set up so we can get a free public education. Anyone can get an education if they want one.

Traditional schools are not the only way to learn. There are fashion design schools, technical schools, vocational schools, church schools, charter schools, and apprenticeship programs. Current technology has developed many on-line opportunities as well. No one has to take the same path to learning.

We learn from daily activities. Children learn respect for others in the way they interact with their playmates. We all learn how to get along with others by participating in clubs, churches, and social organizations.

How many times have you said, "I didn't know that?" and are truly amazed at what you just learned? That joy is yours for all of your life.

Epictetus the Greek philosopher, whose philosophy of Stoicism emphasized freedom, morality, and humanity said, "Only the educated are free."

The educated are free to make choices that affect their daily lives.

The one constant in education is reading. Read everything you can to expand your horizons. I read that if you read a book a month on any one subject for three years you would become a world expert. I do not know if that is true but think of the possibilities! Reading transports you to faraway places - running of the bulls at Spain's annual festival of San Fermin in Pamplona (Navarre, Spain), sailing the seas with Captain Ahab, and exploring the Amazon jungle or the secrets of the Nile. Discover the world through newspapers, magazines, periodicals and books – fiction and nonfiction and on-line. Reading introduces and familiarizes you with issues that affect you and your future.

David Cox said. "If you can read and don't, you are illiterate by choice."

Next, secure your financial health. Sound financial decisions play a huge role in how you invest in your future. We live in a credit/consumer driven society that shouts – BUY NOW PAY LATER!! Growing up my grandmother used to tell us to save for what we wanted because it did not make sense paying any "carrying charges". That was good advice that unfortunately I ignored. I was caught in that buy now cycle for years. I faithfully paid my creditors on time with minimal payments and was happy that I had "good credit". I finally saw the light and eliminated my consumer debt. Get out of debt!!

Another crucial element in securing your financial health is to save a portion of your paycheck. Pay yourself each month just like paying a bill. It does not matter in the beginning how much. Just start the habit of saving. What a great investment in your future. There are many reputable institutions that can help you invest you savings. I will leave that discussion to them.

Finally, invest in your community. This idea supports your connection with society at-large. The Bible says, "...we reap what we sow". To invest in your community is a philosophy that creates a cycle that refreshes and sustains the community. When the community prospers so does the constituents. And you as a constituent will also reap the benefits.

John Donne wrote "No man is an island, entire of itself; every man is a piece of the continent, a part of the main…"

You should develop your talent and determine how to use it to help others. Give freely of your time and knowledge and the community that you are helping will become better and you will become better. You can look in your own past and see people that have invested their time in you. Remember the teachers, clergy and relatives that have helped you to learn and improve. The same responsibility is passed on to you.

Volunteering is a way to help others and learn more about you. My daughter, Cescili, as a freshman in high school volunteered at the local hospital to be a Candy Striper. Her volunteer experience expanded her interest in medicine and she pursued a medical career. She is now a doctor of Obstetrics and Gynecology. Her volunteering was an activity that helped her nurture her interests and what an investment in her future!!

Time spent in education, financial health and community service will secure a handsome return your future.

3

Values to Live By

Values mean different things to different people. Everyone has their own idea of what values mean. The definition may depend on if you are talking about family values, American values, personal values or "old time values". Heads start nodding in a knowing fashion when values are mentioned.

Allen Cox said, "Values are guiding devices to enhance our ability to achieve our purpose."

How would you answer the following questions in determining what you value?

What personal convictions do I have?
What rules guide my life?
What shapes my life?
What is significant in my life?
What do I represent?
What do I need to fulfill my passion and purpose?

Your values must reflect what you believe. You cannot be passionate and purposeful if you believe on thing and do another. Stick to your values no matter the resistance.

There are two types of values: Values we live by and values we aspire to. They are differentiated by our personal behavior. If I profess that I value a healthy lifestyle while exercising and eating nutritious meals then I am living that healthy lifestyle value. However, if I am sedentary and eat junk foods then the healthy personal lifestyle value is one that I aspire to.

Honesty and truth are values that my Mother taught me at a young age. Of course, she did not call them values. She called them "doing what was right". I was a good student and enjoyed going to school. I recall an afternoon in fifth grade taking a history test and for some reason could not figure out the answers. Unconsciously, I turned my head and looked at the test of the student to my left. When I realized what I had done, I looked up at the teacher but she had not seen me. I felt guilty. I felt so guilty that I stopped taking the test and turned it in. I told the teacher that I had cheated. I went back to my desk and put my head down. In a movie of the week I might have gotten a second chance for being honest. In real life I failed the history test but, I passed my Mother's test – "doing what's right". I made sure I was better prepared for history thereafter.

The following exercise has a list of possible values. The list on the next two pages is designed to help you identify your values and determine your highest priority values. This list is not comprehensive so feel free to add your own.

Step one – Choose twenty values.
Step two – Next choose your top ten values.
Step three – Choose your top five.
Step four – Rank the top five.

You will have your top five priority values.

Achievement	Knowledge
Advancement	Leadership
Affection	Loyalty
Belief System	Love
Challenging problems	Money
Character	Meaningful work

Creativity	Originality
Competition	Organization
Commitment	Patience
Citizenship	Passion
Discipline	Peace
Discovery	Prestige
Education	Persistence
Empathy	Personal strength
Environmental awareness	Pleasure
Entertainment	Personal development
Fame	Power
Financial Security	Playing Sports
Friendship	Role Model
Family	Safety
Honesty	Showing expertise
Helping others	Spirituality
Inspiring others	Stability
Respect	Simplicity
Integrity	Tolerance
Independence	Truth
Inner harmony	Wisdom
Introspection	Working alone
Justice	Working with others

The last step is to determine what type of values you have prioritized. Do you live these values or do you aspire to these values? If you live them, that is great. If you aspire to them, you now have a guide.

4

Imagination is Creation

Imagination may be described in two ways: a space not limited by our sense or reason that we can unquestioningly embrace or a capacity for ground-breaking thinking and creative expression.

Children make-believe all the time and imagine all kinds of possibilities. We should reach back to that time of endless possibilities and grab the wishes we passionately longed for and make them happen in our lives. The fun part of imagination is that there are no rules but the ones you create. If you can imagine a green sky with blue trees and red grass, then so be it.

"I paint things as I think them, not as I see them"

Pablo Picasso

I don't remember ever having an imaginary friend like a six-foot tall, invisible rabbit, in the movie classic *"Harvey"* starring Jimmy Stewart, but I had an active imagination. My father was in the Air force and at one time did in-flight refueling. I imagined what it would be like to be in the air doing his job or what it was like to fly the airplane itself. My mother, when I was in elementary school, subscribed to a monthly National Geographic program that sent slides for a manual viewfinder. Every month my sister and I were transported to faraway places like Egypt, London, China or Africa. I learned a lot and imagined what adventures I would have in these exotic locales. Later, when I fell in love with comic books, I became Superman or Mr. Fantastic or Daredevil and yes I dreamed I could fly.

"Creativity represents a miraculous coming together of the uninhibited energy of the child with its apparent opposite and enemy the sense of order imposed on the disciplined adult intelligence."

Norman Podhoretz

Wilbur and Orville Wright of Dayton, Ohio believed in human powered flight – they imagined a man could fly. On Dec. 17, 1903, with Orville at the controls, the Flyer, a flying machine of spruce, ash and muslin, lifted off from Kitty Hawk and flew 120 ft. The seed of that dream has grown into air travel today that more than likely is beyond the Wright brothers' wildest dreams.

"The man who has no imagination has no wings".

Muhammad Ali

Can you imagine a box outside of a bank that will give you money? In 1939, Luther George Simjian started patenting an earlier and not-so-successful version of an ATM machine called Bankmatic. Don Wetzel, however was the inventor of the modern automated teller machines. Can you imagine what it would be like today without the convenience of an ATM?

We are all blessed with a spark of creation. We have the ability to imagine our future, create outcomes that we want and imagine some more!!

"Everything that is new or uncommon raises a pleasure in the imagination, because it fills the soul with an agreeable surplus, gratifies its curiosity, and gives it an idea of which it was not before possessed."

Joseph Addeson

Try this exercise: Imagine something that you passionately desire. Examine that outcome using all your senses.

How do you describe it?
What sensation do you get when you touch it?
How does it sound?
How does it smell or taste?
Is it clear in your mind?
Do you still want it?
If so, then go for it!!

You can use this exercise or make up one on your own. Remember, imagination knows no boundaries.

5

Navigate through failure

Failure is good. There are four elements that will help you understand how to navigate through failure.

1) You have taken a risk or attempted a task
2) You know that approach does not work
3) You gain a different perspective
4) You have the opportunity to start again

The first element – You have taken a risk or attempted a task means you are active. You knew what you wanted and attempted to get it. Theodore Roosevelt, the 26th President of the United States of America, in his *Citizenship in a Republic* speech at the Sorbonne, Paris characterizes this best when he told his audience:

"It is not the critic who counts, not the man who points out how the strong man stumbles, or where the doer of deeds could have done better. The credit belongs to the man who is actually in the arena, whose face is marred by dust and sweat and blood, who strives valiantly, who errs and comes up short again and again, because there is no effort without error or shortcoming, but who knows the great enthusiasms, the great devotions, who spends himself for a worthy cause; who at best, knows in the end the triumph of high achievement and who, at worst, if he fails at least he fails while daring greatly, so

that his place shall never be with those cold and timid souls who know neither victory nor defeat."

The second element – You know that approach does not work. In the words of Bill Murray in the movie *Stripes* – *"That's a fact Jack."* Thomas Alva Edison was asked how it felt to have failed 10,000 times before inventing and electric lamp. Edison corrected the inquiry by saying he had not failed 10,000 times but he had found 10,000 ways not to invent the electric lamp.

"It is on our failures that we base a new and different and better success."

Havelock Ellis

The third element - You gain a different perspective. Failure is in the eye of the beholder. My son, RT, played cornerback on his Pee Wee football team. One Saturday morning he was playing a team that ran the power sweep like the Old Cleveland Browns when Jim Brown was a star in the AFL. Sweep after sweep the team would come around the corner and RT would get wiped out. RT and his teammates were only able to stop the sweep a few times. I was standing on the sidelines trying to figure out how to console him for his failure to contain or slow down the power sweep. The game mercifully ended and I waited for RT to come off the field. I prepared a little pep talk about trying his best and better luck next time. When he got to me, I asked him about the other team's power sweep and what did he think? He looked at me and said, "I know why they were running the sweeps all day." I was curious and asked him to explain. He said, "They ran the sweep because they were afraid to pass against me." Wow what we learn out of the mouths of babes. I learned a lesson that day.

The fourth element – You have the opportunity to start again. There is the old adage - if at first you don't succeed, try and try again. The difference between failing and succeeding could be one more try. Abraham Lincoln, the 16th President of the United States of America embodied the fourth element.

Failed in business	1831
Defeated in Legislature	1832
Failed in business again	1833
Defeated for Speaker	1838
Defeated for election	1840
Defeated for Congress	1848
Defeated for Senate	1855
Defeated for Vice President	1856
Defeated for Senate	1858
Elected President	1860

How many times must you fail before you win? Only enough until you win.

6

Goals - GOing After Life's Successes

Goals help you achieve what you desire. This is your success. Going after life's success is striving toward your dreams, your passion and your purpose. I define going after life's success with three elements:

a) Develop a clear goal
b) Acquire the resources to make it happen
c) Relentlessly focus resources on your goal

Your goals must reflect your values. When your goals and values are in sync your chances of living both are exponentially enhanced.

The first element of going after life's success is a **GREAT©** goal. This is an acronym to guide you in setting goals: Gratifying, Reasonable, Explicit, Achievable, and Time-based.

Gratifying: Your goal should fulfill your desire. Its completion should bring satisfaction. This aspect of your goal creates the motivation and the drive to complete the tasks necessary to claim your prize. The reward is sweet and you are pleased. When I was a youngster the idea of making the school basketball team gave me goose bumps. When I finally made the team it was gratifying!!

Reasonable: Your goal should be within the bounds of your common sense. In other words, whatever you choose should make sense to you. Remember, you will determine what your goals are and what they mean to you. In my case, making the basketball team made sense to me based on my experiences on the playground. I grew up and played well against guys who made my school's basketball team. I figured when the time came for me to go out for the team I could make it also.

Explicit: This step is your first step. Your goal should be definite. You should be specific in what you want. Just like your values assessment, you need to know what your goal looks like. You should easily be able to recognize it when you achieve it. Next, write it down. Writing your goal down is commitment. How does it look on paper? How does it sound when you say it out loud? You can review it, revise it and hone it down until it is exactly what you want. My goal was to make the school team. The words "making the school team" were melodic to me.

Achievable: You goal can be accomplished by mental or physical effort. Your ability to think, learn or work hard will make your goal possible.

"Leaders aren't born they are made. And they are made just like anything else, through hard work. And that's the price we'll have to pay to achieve that goal, or any goal."

Vince Lombardi

I believed that if I ran enough and practiced my ball handling, free throws, and jump shooting that I could make the team. I knew as much about the game as my peers so, I felt mentally prepared to play.

Time based: Your goal should have an end date. If lifelong learning is your goal then you do not need an end date. However, the majority of goals should have a completion time. Time based also contains an element of measurement. You need both so you can gauge if you are progressing toward completion of your goal. The last cut sheet would be posted a week after tryouts. There was no doubt when my goal would be complete. I was still there going into the last week so I was progressing toward my goal.

The second element of going after life's success is **acquiring the resources to make it happen**. What resources do you need to make your goal happen? You could seek help from others. You may determine you need specific machinery or materials. My resources for making the school basketball team were a basketball, a basketball court with rim, a pair of sneakers and the neighborhood guys to play against.

The third element of going after life's success is to **relentlessly focus resources on your goal**. You must focus your management of people, machinery and materials in a matter that completes your goal. So, I had a basketball, a dirt court with basketball rim, my sneakers and my boys to play against. I played every day after school and practiced and practiced and practiced to make the school team.

Now comes, as Paul Harvey would say, the rest of the story. The thought of making the team was gratifying. I was reasonable in thinking I could do what my peers had done. My goal was explicit – to make the school team. I was physically and mentally ready and I knew when it could happen.

Here's what happened:

Eighth grade – did not make team.

Ninth grade – did not make team.

Tenth grade – finally made junior varsity. I did not play much.

Eleventh grade – made Junior varsity and started every game.

Twelfth grade – made varsity and started every game. I earned All City, District and Regional honors.

College – played four years. I earned All-Conference three years, honorable mention All-America my senior year and was inducted in Case Western Reserve's Basketball Hall of Fame.

Post College – I tried out for the Cleveland Cavaliers – did not make the team. But oh what a run! And all I wanted to do initially was make the junior high basketball team.

Everyone can reach his or her goals. Everyone can embrace going after life's success.

7

Listen

We are Promoters and Explorers. We promote our ideas with emotion. We explore the world around us by listening for meaning and answers. Promotion and exploration are yin and yang on the coin of communication and learning. Promoters talk, explorers listen. Both are needed for communication but learning comes from listening.

"A wise man listening to a fool will learn more than a fool listening to a wise man."

Anonymous

Most people prefer promoting. They never take a breath as they promote their ideas. Are there times that we must promote an idea? Of course there are. Even so, we should explore what we are sending and what is being heard.

Explorers know listening is a choice. Active listening focuses on a message and its meaning. Unconscious listening is only hearing. Hearing is involuntary. Hearing is a physical sensation created by an external stimulus. We are bombarded by sounds around us like traffic, television, conversations, construction and more. We must prioritize what we listen to so that we don't miss something important. Take this conversation for instance.

Husband (concerned): "What's wrong honey?"

Wife (sniffling): You didn't get me a birthday present."
Husband (perplexed): "But you told me not to get you anything this year."
Wife (innocently): "That's what I said, but you know what I meant."
Husband (getting his coat): "I'll be right back."

The husband heard what his wife was saying but he was not listening. Technically he may have been right, but his inability to pick up the subtle message behind his wife's words caught him off guard.

"When making personal decisions, listen to what your head says; then listen to what your heart says. If they differ follow your heart! Whenever you listen to you heart, you listen to that part of you that is most interested in your well-being.

Anonymous

What are a few obstacles to listening? Imagine we are sitting in a training seminar, or lecture hall or even in church. We daydream. We are not interested in the subject. We focus on the speaker's clothing or delivery. We are distracted by outside noise or conversations. We feel the room is not right. We are impatient or self-absorbed.

Listening for understanding is a learned skill. Explorers use two types of feedback to check understanding – statement confirmation and questioning for clarity.

Statement confirmation is restating what you think the speaker is saying. Explorers are able to paraphrase the speaker's words to the speaker's satisfaction.

Questioning for clarification is asking for additional information to clarify your view of the speaker's message. Explorers use this method to double-check their understanding.

One-on-one statement confirmation and questioning for clarity is a quicker process than in a group setting. Statement confirmation and questioning for clarity in a group setting may entail taking notes, reviewing for restatement and asking questions later.

Statement confirmation and questioning for clarity does not mean you agree with the speaker. It means that you are seeking understanding of the message.

You as a Promoter can refine your ideas by becoming an Explorer. Prepare your audience by asking for active listening. Tell your audience you will ask them to paraphrase your idea, you will open the floor for clarifying questions, expect feedback on whether your idea makes sense and entertain how they would improve your idea. Can you see what happens? You become an Explorer. You actively listen to feedback. You now can switch roles back to Promoter with a better chance of presenting your idea in terms that makes sense to your audience.

You have created the coin of communication and learning.

Take time to listen. Often times, the things we seek are right underneath our noses. Don't miss out on your blessing because it isn't packaged the way that you expect.

Anonymous

8

Inspire Others

You can be a role model and/or a mentor. A role model projects behavior that is emulated by others. This definition does not determine whether the behavior is good or bad. We learn from positive role models how to live. We learn what no to do from negative role models.

How can you be a role model? You have a special talent that is yours to share with others. Project a clear picture of who you are, what is important to you and the direction you are headed. Awaken the expectations of a good life in people around you. Your behavior is an example observed by those around you. As such, you are a walking advertisement of your values, your goals and your life.

"Be such a man and live such a life, that if every man were such as you, and every life a life like yours, this earth would be God's paradise."
Philip Brooks American Episcopal Bishop

There are a number of people who are or have been role models in my life. My parents, Russell and Elizabeth, were the most important. My father modeled the discipline of military duty and pride for his work in the Air Force. He would rise every morning at 5:30 am and prepare for work. He was clean-shaven, shoes were always shined, uniform crisply pressed, fed (that was Mother's doing) and out the door by 6:30 am. My mother was open and loving and modeled how to treat others with respect and how to anticipate and merit respect from others.

I joined the Boy Scouts in sixth grade. I wore my uniform as proudly as my father wore his. My Scout leaders were Ed Badgett, Charles Howell and Charles Dardie. These three men met with us weekly and took us camping once a month. They taught us the ways of scouting and more importantly how to be young men. We did not think of them as role models and mentors but they were.

Society has elevated athletes to celebrity status and role models. The Nike Corporation ran a successful advertising campaign calling on viewers to "Be like Mike". Mike, of course, is the Hall of Fame basketball player Michael Jordan. Charles Barkley, voted as one of the 50 greatest players in NBA history, on the other hand said,

"Just because I can dunk a basketball doesn't mean I should raise your kids."

What a contrast in looking at the sports hero as a role model. Michael Jordan has accepted his status as a role model. Charles Barkley, on the other hand, does not see himself as a role model. Both, however, project behavior that others copy.

How can you be a mentor? A mentor offers knowledge and expertise (your special talent) on a given topic to someone (mentee) who wants a hands on approach.

There are different types of mentoring – business and social. Business mentoring could put together a senior management executive with a high performing junior executive or a new worker in a department with a veteran employee. Social mentoring one-on-one like Big Brothers Big Sisters demonstrates how adults can help children at risk overcome day-to-day challenges.

A business or social mentor must do the following in order to establish a mentoring relationship:

Be perceived as being able to help. A mentee must know that what you bring to the table (your special talent) will help them. Essentially, you are letting them know who you are, why you are there, how you can help and to set expectations. Your own self disclosure will help your mentee feel comfortable. You should gather information from your mentee that will help you gain rapport and establish a relationship.

Create a trusting environment that offers and receives open feedback. A trusting environment is a two way street. Mentor and mentee should feel at ease with healthy discussions that further learning.

Challenge and encourage learning that supports lessons learned from missteps. Sometimes great lessons are learned from trial and error. A mentor must allow the mentee to fail but encourage and challenge them to stand up and to start again.

No matter who you are or where you are in life you can inspire others.

"This is the beginning of a new day. You have been given this day to use as you will. You can waste it or use it for good. What you do today is important because you are exchanging a day of your life for it. When tomorrow comes, this day will be gone forever; in its place is something you have left behind... let it be something good.

Author unknown

9

Friendship can last a lifetime

Friends are great to have. What more could one ask? True friendships are rare relationships that I wish were more common. Friendships are warm and comforting. The gathering of friends is a gathering of support and hope and fun.

Our friends can help us see the many possibilities that are available to us. Each friend's opinion shares a different perspective of who we are and what we can do. Being around others that you can trust and confide in builds self-confidence and can relieve a lot of stress or anxiety.

Friendship comes in many forms. There are friends that you talk to consistently. These friends are up to date on the latest everything in your life. You trade information and gossip daily or every couple of days. You either see them through the week or talk on the phone. I wrote this poem to describe my friends.

My friends are treasures beyond traditional measures
No room filled with gold has the volume enough to hold
Their value and what they mean to me

Friends are reflections that mirror my life's directions
Wherever I go wherever I rest I always know
I will find them or they will find me

My friends are allies who won't tolerate any lies
Our truth is our pact fashioning the way we act
My friends who are favored forever

My friends are treasures beyond traditional measures
Wherever I go wherever I rest I always know
Their value – I can feel them – my friends

There are friends that your talk to infrequently. However, when you do speak, it seems like it was only yesterday that you last spoke to each other. The warmth and comfort comes flowing back and you start up wherever you left off.

Then there are the friends yet to be made - the future friends. The future holds many possibilities among which are new friendships. People who share an interest or vocation will come into your life. Some of these people will become favored companions – friends.

Each friend represents a world in us, a world possibly not born until they arrive, and it is only by this meeting that a new world is born.
Anais Nin

You cultivate friendships by being a friend. Sound simple doesn't it? That means that friendship is a two way street. Your end of the friendship is important. You must be supportive, warm and comforting. You have to listen and be patient. Sometimes you have to be constructively critical to help a friend. We have to encourage our friends to be their best selves. Being a friend means working through rumors or misunderstandings. This will mean giving a friend the benefit of the doubt until you talk to them.

Do friendships last a lifetime? Is there a time to quietly end a friendship? The type of friendship I have described to this point can last a lifetime. There may come a time to walk away from a friendship if your friend is one who:

Always makes jokes at your expense
Gets jealous when you are doing well
Only call you as a last resort for activities
Always seems negative or is complaining about something
Tells you about plans they have made and leaves you out
Only talks but never listens
Wants to be your only friend and you're their only friend

Doesn't sound much like friendship does it? You must be on guard to not fall into those behaviors yourself. So what do you do if your friendship is no longer healthy? Talk to your friend. Explain what bothers you and see if your friend understands. People sometimes unknowingly act a certain way. They may not recognize a problem because we have accepted the behavior for so long it seems natural. Speak your piece then use some active listening. You may be able to salvage a friendship. Otherwise it may be time to "breakup" with that friend.

Friends in your life are like pillars on your porch. Sometimes they hold you up and sometimes they lean on you. Sometimes it's just enough to know they're standing by.

Anonymous

Here is an item to add to your to do list if you have one. If you do not have a list then you can start one with this.

1) Make a list of all your friends.
2) Call them.

10

Examine Leadership Principles

Leadership is fluid. Leadership blends the components of vision, power, events and followership (the willingness of others to follow). A leader describes a vision of the future that benefits his followers and enhances their idea of what is possible. In this lesson leaders can be substituted with managers while followers can be substituted with employees, congregation, or even consumers.

President John F Kennedy was the first president that I was aware of as a child. Foremost in my mind as a child, was his presence during the Cuban missile crisis. I did not recognize it then as leadership but that is what it was. On another occasion President Kennedy described a vision, when he gave a special message to a joint Session of Congress on urgent national needs.

First, I believe this nation should commit itself to achieving the goal, before the decade is out, of landing a man on the moon and returning him safely to earth…I believe we should go to the moon. But…there is no sense in agreeing or desiring the United States take an affirmative position in outer space, unless we are prepared to do the work and bear the burdens to make it successful.

September 12, 1962, at Rice University, Houston Texas, President Kennedy spoke on the nation's space effort.

Many years ago the great British explorer George Mallory, who was to die on Mount Everest, was asked why de want to climb it. He said, "Because it is there." Well, space is there and we're going to climb it, and the moon and the planets are, and new hopes for knowledge and peace are there!

Seven years later, on July 21, 1969, the vision of President Kennedy was realized when Neil A Armstrong landed on the moon and returned safely. Kennedy galvanized a nation using his vision and charismatic skills. He did not define how to get to the moon. He created an environment (the space appropriation bill) that let his people figure it out. The end goal was clear however. Get to the moon and back safely.

The next component of leadership is power. The power component is: the ability of the leader to influence the behavior of his followers and/or the willingness of the followers to accept influence based on the perception of the leader's power.

Power described by John French and Bertram Raven in their book, *"Bases of Social Power, Studies in Social Power"*, consisted of five elements of power: Referent, expert, legitimate, coercive and reward. It is widely recognized that the five bases of social power influence business relationships as well as personal relationships.

Referent power can be described as "emulation is the highest form of flattery". The leader is seen as possessing positive qualities. People identify and mold themselves after the leader. An example of referent power is when it is used in commercial advertising. Nike created the "Be Like Mike" campaign starring Michael Jordan. Consumers identified with Jordan's charisma and patterned themselves after him by buying replicas of his jersey and his shoes and his underwear. Jordan had a receding hairline as a young adult. He shaved his head and young men all over the country followed suit with the bald look. Now that is referent power!

Expert power is influence by one who has special knowledge or skills. Others will follow because they hold the perception that the expert knows the best way to do something. Our perception of medical doctors and lawyers are an example of expert power.

The influence of experts is confined to their area of expertise. One would not expect a medical doctor to explain the intricacies of home construction or an attorney to troubleshoot your laptop computer.

Legitimate power is acceptance in a work environment that managers or supervisors are entitled to make decisions based on job title or authority given by the corporation. This power is confined to the area that others deem legitimate. Your boss may have influence over you at work but not in your home.

Coercive power is negative leadership based on fear. Followers believe in the ability of the leader to punish and enforce consequences if they do not comply with requests on demand. Most of us have seen how a bully behaves whether socially or at work. The bully creates fear with threats and the occasional beating to keep those around him in line. Coercive power works until fear is replaced or ignored. Ralphie Parker and his buddies in the movie *"A Christmas Story"* were constantly being bullied. One afternoon after school Ralphie was frustrated. He had received a C+ on his written report. That combined with the fact that his decoder ring (the one he had daily drank Ovaltine for weeks and waited anxiously to get in the mail) decoded a message that was a blatant commercial put him at wit's end. The bully on the block confronted Ralphie on the way home. Ralphie snapped. Ralphie tackled the bully and pummeled him until his mother pulled him off of the bully. Needless to say the coercive power of that bully was diminished not only for Ralphie but also for the other kids in the neighborhood.

Reward power is the ability to distribute wealth that others see as valuable. The power is enhanced when followers see expected behaviors are approved and rewarded. Companies use bonuses, commissions, trips and other incentives as rewards. A well placed comment or simple praise can enhance one's reward power. Employees are more willing to "keep their noses to the grindstone" when they know their work is appreciated and will be rewarded.

Events can create leaders. Urban renewal was a great concern in my neighborhood on the West side of Akron, Ohio in the late 80's. The city of Akron was acquiring land by eminent domain to expand the local hospital and Telephone Company. City officials called a neighborhood meeting to discuss the expansion plans and the relocation of the residents. The meeting was chaotic.

All parties wanted to be heard. Our city councilman and council person at large could not calm the residents. The city officials were following an agenda that did not resonate with the resident. Talk about a time for leadership!!

I was not thinking about leadership at the time but I knew I had to do something. I probably rose for altruistic reasons because my Mother's home was being affected. I got everyone's attention. I explained to the city officials and the residents that we had three different sets of concern. We had homeowners (my Mother), landlords and tenants with questions. The answers would be different for each group. I suggested that the meeting be divided into three groups and specific concerns of each group be addressed separately. All parties agreed and the meeting continued in smaller groups and the issues were worked out.

Why did the city officials and residents listen to me? The group was looking for answers and at that moment I had a plan that would benefit all parties. The group was willing to follow my lead because they saw the benefit to them. That event created a need for leadership and I temporarily filled the void until everything was on track.

Leaders need followership. The willingness of others to follow is what allows leaders to lead.

"True leadership must be for the benefit of the followers, not the enrichment of the leaders."

Robert Townsend Up the Organization

Leaders understand that the group must benefit from his vision. The leader cannot take the credit for the work the group has done. One's leadership style may vary depending on circumstances but in the end, the group (employees, followers, consumers or friends) must prosper.

Leadership is fluid. Leadership can be learned and effective when one understands the principles of vision, power, events and followership.

11

Wise choices

Life is a series of choices. Every day you are confronted with choices that affect your life. Your choices should connect with your values and goals. A quick filter will determine whether a current decision is compatible with your values and goals. Sometimes a short term decision may obstruct a long term goal. Relevant, reliable information supports good decision making. Always consider the source of your information and whether it is timely, credible and unbiased. With all your facts together you can prioritize your options, analyze the consequences of each one and make your choice.

Choices can be categorized as technical or social decisions.

Technical choices are commonplace, matter-of-fact, everyday decisions. Should I eat pancakes or eggs for breakfast? Should I wear the red or the blue shirt? Do you want to wait until the sale item comes in or buy something else? These choices do not include right or wrong. They represent alternatives, preferences, or availability. You can easily handle these choices by: gathering facts, list advantages versus disadvantages and go with the best option.

When I was in the seventh grade in Ohio I took a wood shop class. I started building a bookcase for my Grandmother who lived in Mississippi. Basketball tryouts started and I had to make a choice between trying out for the team and finishing the bookcase. I chose to finish the bookcase. It was a technical choice because there was no right or wrong answer. Unfortunately I never made the junior high basketball team. I also had not considered how I was going to get a five-foot bookcase to my Grandmother. It never made it to Mississippi but I never regretted building it for her.

Social choices represent the concept of ethical decision-making. Ethics are principles of right or wrong. A decision passes judgment on an issue under consideration. Ethics is a study of the general nature of morals and the specific moral choices to be made by the individual in his relationship with others. Social choices as ethical decisions imply making judgments based on a moral code and how they affect you and others.

Unlike technical choices there is a moral significance to social choices. What we choose and how we choose to make those decisions should be filtered through the ethical principles of: caring, citizenship, fairness, respect, responsibility and trustworthiness.

My greatest counselor was my Mother. She had a way of saying things that made me understand without sounding preachy. One of her pearls on choice was, "Whatever you do in the dark will sooner or later see the light of day". What does that mean? It meant the choices that are made when no one can see you will eventually be revealed. Also, would my choices hold up under scrutiny? If my character, upbringing, and integrity were held up for inspection would I stand tall or be embarrassed?

Social choices as ethical decisions are made personally and in business every day. CEOs, front line managers, and employees have to make choices that affect others. The following questions can help you make ethical social choices.

A perfect world would mean these questions would not be necessary or there would be no issues to making ethical social choices. We live in a real world and sometimes there are excuses to why we choose what we choose.

PERSONAL	BUSINESS
1. Is it legal?	1. Is it legal?
2. Does it coincide with my personal goals and values?	2. Does it comply with my company values?
3. Is it the right thing to do?	3. Does it make sense if everyone is treated this way?
4. How will it affect my family, friends and others?	4. How does it affect our stockholders and employees
5. How will I feel?	5. How will I feel?
6. What would my Mother think?	6. Can the decision withstand public scrutiny?

I Want to Fit In

We want to be a part of a something. Wanting to be part of social groups can get in the way of making ethical social choices. Headlines from the newspaper regale how socially accepted groups – college fraternities/sororities and socially un-accepted groups – gangs make unethical social choices to fit in.

Hazing is an illegal and dangerous act. Yet across America, "pledges" accept this behavior to fit in. Despite deaths, injuries, lawsuits and public disapproval from public and the fraternity/sorority hierarchy the behavior persists. It is brutal and unnecessary to take a beating to prove oneself. There are those who want to fit it and others who are willing to accommodate that desire.

Initiation rites into gangs require socially unethical choices like committing a crime in front of gang witnesses. Young men and women are "keeping it real" by disregarding societies moral code and making unethical social choices to fit in.

The Easy Way Out

The easy way out is a quick decision without thought or a conscious decision to avoid tough consequences. The KISS (Keep it Simple Simon) theory is used on problems that require more thought.

Over simplification of an issue can lead to unworkable solutions. Not every decision has a complex set of elements but, forethought and exploration enhances your ability to make an ethical social choice.

A group of boys were playing sand lot baseball. The boy at bat hit a long fly ball that crashed through a neighbor's window. All the boys scatter as soon as they hear the window breaking. Why did they run? The probably thought about being in trouble, having to pay for a new window and decided to get away. It was the easiest thing to do.

"Honest hearts produce honest actions."

Brigham Young

Everybody's Doing It

The mantra "everybody's doing it" is another excuse that is a barrier to ethical social choice. One summer when I was in high school I witnessed protests in my community. Those protests turned into riots with looting, chaos, and destruction. The initial comments from the "protesters" were about the Vietnam War, how they were treated and how the "Man" was keeping them down. Before you could holler "No justice no peace" people were coming from all over breaking storefront windows and looting the neighborhood businesses. When asked why they were looting the stores the comment was "everybody's doing it".

There is an old story of a parent talking to his teenager about the teen's behavior. The teenager shrugged off the parent with the reply "everybody's doing it". The parent responded with, "If everyone is jumping off a bridge, would you?"

Robert Bennett summarized wise choices when he said:

Your life is the sum result of all the choices you make, both consciously and unconsciously. If you can control the process of choosing, you can take control of all aspects of your life. You can find the freedom that comes from being in charge of yourself.

Choose wisely.

12

It is about You

This is about you and you only. Indulge yourself for a little while.

Examination of You is an opportunity to evaluate your inner self. All too often, we live outside ourselves engaged in the world around us. Images and sound bites from print and electronic media wash over us. Opinions from friends and family bombard us from every direction. We unconsciously set up defense mechanisms to protect or at least filter through these external stimuli and do not reserve time for our inner selves.

Our personal beliefs are important. But what are they? Our personal feelings shape how we think of things and how those "things" will affect us. In some societies meditation is a form of introspection. Setting aside some time to contemplate and examine what is. Not what is important or what is coming up for the day. But what is…period. Be it about life, love, self or nothing.

Meaningful meditation and contemplation of self is personal and sets a foundation for living a life with passion and purpose. Think of setting aside time to examine what is around you. How do you feel about the current world tragedy or the homeless in your town? How are your relationships? Do you feel about issues the way you want to feel or are your feelings a reflection of how others think you should feel?

Meditation and contemplation overcome confusion that creates dependence on others (external) to define what you think or who you are (internal). Ignorance creates dependence on others to define who we are or what we think. That is a high price to pay. These methods of self-examination can help you develop a balanced perspective of your worldview. Your values and who you are counterbalance the world around you. You can feel confident in addressing external issues because of your internal peace.

Some people may be afraid to explore meditation and contemplation. Accepting the truth, about your inner self, may create energy to change if you do not like what you discover. Many people do not want to change. They enjoy a routine that does not make them think or contemplate anything. Fear can give us an edge if used properly. There are bumps in the road to slow us down but you cannot let them stop you. Looking at your self is liberating. You cannot deny who you are. I am sure there are many frustrated and unhappy people because they deny who they are. You can change if you do not like who you are. That is a benefit of meditation and contemplation. You can look at yourself honestly and then decide if you want to change. There is no perfection in this life so there is room for improvement. By the same token if you like what you see then enjoy. Don't be afraid to stay the way you are.

Meditation and contemplation helps you harmonize your external stimuli with an inner focus. Many people conjure up an image of sitting cross-legged and chanting when they think of meditation. That can be the beginning of a method of meditation however; meditation or contemplation can be what you want them to be. There is no right or wrong way to do either.

There are many benefits to meditation and contemplation. The benefits include the aforementioned and the following but are not limited to: self-healing, relaxation, improved sleep, inner peace and resolution to external problems.

Meditation is an opportunity to promote balance and harmony. Balance and harmony are demonstrated by the notion of yin/yang, dark/light, good/evil, plus/minus or up and down. These are all connected and there is no harmony when one is out of sync with the other. Your life is comprised of external and internal elements:

chaos (external) and peace (internal). Meditation helps you develop a balance.

The following is a method to meditate. It is not the only method but it is a beginning.

Choose to open yourself to the benefits of meditation. Choose to release any anxiety or restlessness that may surround you.

Choose a location where you will not be disturbed. Dress in comfortable clothing that is not confining or restrictive. Sit in a position that is comfortable. Do not lie down because you could fall asleep.

Let you tension drain away and relax. Focus inward to think of nothing and breathe. Breathe naturally and let your breathing become the focus of your meditation to the exclusion of all other thoughts.

You will become aware of how much you think about. When your mind wanders refocus on your breathing with the goal of nothingness – no thoughts, no worries, no anxieties. Your meditation will take on a different energy when you achieve this state.

Try this meditation for 15 or 20 minutes daily. As with all things you get better with practice. Your results are yours. There is not right or wrong.

Contemplation is an internal focus on external issues. The initial preparation is the same but working on a different result. Contemplation is focusing on an issue to open the possibilities for clarification and/or resolution.

The following is a method of contemplation.

Choose to release any anxiety or restlessness that may surround you.

Choose a location where you will not be disturbed. Dress in comfortable clothing that is not confining or restrictive. Sit in a position that is comfortable. Do not lie down because you could fall asleep.

Let your tension drain away and relax. The first part of your contemplation is to examine your topic. Focus inward to think of your topic and breathe naturally. If your mind wanders, refocus on your breathing with the goal of seeing your topic.

Once you reach the essence of your topic – let it go and open yourself to the many possibilities of clarification and resolution. Let the possibilities flow.

There is no right or wrong. There may or may not be an epiphany. The odds to receive some possibilities are in your favor because you are open to possibilities.

Try this meditation for 15 or 20 minutes daily. As with all things you get better with practice.

Some new ideas may flow into your consciousness during your contemplation time and you may wish to retain them. Keep a notepad or journal by your side. When you are done, write in your journal those things you wish to remember. Do it daily and you will be surprised at the amazing reflections you will compile.

Children are dependent on others because the world is brand new. Once we reach an age of intellectual awareness and separation, we want to take control of our lives. We as introspective people can take in the world's messages, balance those messages with our inner peace and be free. Know yourself and be free.

13

Time is on Your side

Time management is recognizing that you can get done what needs to be done. Time is fluid but unchanging. No matter how we approach time, it does not stop. Seconds, minutes, hours, days, months and years steadily march on with or without our consent or input.

Effective time management is the ability to balance our lives. Your ability to balance time for work, play, learning and growth determines how successful you are in life.

There are one hundred and sixty eight (168) hours in a week. How do you use that time? What do you need to accomplish? I have developed the POWERR™ system of time management to help you.

Plan and Prioritize
Overcome Interruptions
Waylay Procrastination
Embrace your plan
Review your plan
Reward your self

Plan and Prioritize

You need to know where you are going and when you have to be there. Do you know what you do all week? This exercise will gather the information needed to make your plan.

1. Create seven daily worksheets
2. List half-hour increments for 12 am to 12 pm.
3. Record your activities in half hour increments
4. Add up hours by activity.

Your 24-hour day can be divided into many subsets with the basic two being either sleep time or waking hours. You may choose from the following list or make your own.

Sleep, recreation, studying, eating reading, intimacy, exercise, watching television, work, baby sitting or driving.

You now have a visual summary and numerical summary of your time. How do you spend most of your time? Are there activities that can be trimmed or expanded? It is your time; use it the way you want to.

Overcome Interruptions

Interruptions come in different forms. How you deal with interruptions will determine more time management issues. Have you ever wondered why the interruptions happen? There is a virus that can overwhelm you quickly if you are not careful. Has this ever happened to you?

Your project is due in four days. You have enough time to complete it if you stay on task. You are now vulnerable to the dreaded office virus called "projectus interruptus". A subtle but insidious infection designed to knock your project off track. The symptoms are:

Your colleague with a fresh cup of coffee in hand, the latest news on everything but your project, sits down, and gets comfortable.

The phone rings with requests for you to: attend a meeting; go to lunch early, or to join someone down the hall for a birthday celebration.

Your opinion becomes invaluable. Everyone has to talk to you right now to solve a problem.

If you catch "projectus interruptus" be prepared to spend long hours and sleepless nights meeting your deadline. There is a strain of this virus that can attack you when you are at home. It is called "home-work interruptus". It works the same way as "projectus" when studying, doing household chores or home improvement projects.

The cure for these curious viruses is a dose of vitamin D^2 - discipline and diplomacy. D^2 enhances your ability to manage your time against all forms of "interruptus". Whether at work or at home, you will be alert to the symptoms and can handle interruptions as they occur. You will recognize the symptoms of "projectus or home-work interruptus" and say no to interruptions. Vitamin D^2 gives you strength to explain to colleagues or friends that you have a project and you can't take a break. You can just say no.

Waylay Procrastination

Interruptions are external while procrastination is internal. We might blame outside forces for interruptions but for procrastination we are the culprits. Procrastination can cause missed deadlines, unfinished projects, and general frustration from not completing assignments.

Take for instance this little court drama on procrastination not published in any law journal. This litigation will later become known as: "The Procrastination Case".

"Hear ye! Hear ye! Please rise for the Honorable Norman Oswald Xkewsis." Judge Xkewsis, an enormous man, enters the courtroom and motions for everyone to be seated.

The judge announces in a voice that shakes the courtroom, *"This is case 13013, Book Publishing Company versus Ima Writer. The defendant has been charged with reckless procrastination. I will hear opening arguments. Ms. Payne you may begin."*

The attorney for BPC stands up from her desk and quickly walks in front of the jury.

"Ladies and gentlemen of the jury, today's case is simple. The defendant, contracted to write a novel, is charged with reckless procrastination. I will show how the defendant found little projects to do around the house to keep from writing. I will show how the defendant sloughed off doing research by trying to conquer the thirty levels of Zoondoff the Magician on her computer. Furthermore, I will show how the defendant watched television during the times she set aside to work on her novel. Ladies and gentleman of the jury I will prove beyond a shadow of a doubt that Ima Writer is guilty of reckless procrastination."

The BPC attorney sits down. The attorney, for Ima Writer, Lou Wilty, stands to begin his opening statement when there is a buzz in the back of the courtroom. Everyone turns to see who is entering the court. When Ima looks she is crestfallen. In walks Harvey Cooper, her home improvement coordinator from the local hardware store, then PP Ferdinand from CompuGames, and lastly the cable guy who explained how to order premium movies on her cable system.

"Order in the court", bellows Judge Xkewsis, *"Order in the court."*

Ima yanks on the arm of her attorney and he bends down toward her. She whispers something in his ear and he nods.

"Your honor, my client would like to plead no contest to the charges of reckless procrastination and throw herself at the mercy of the court."

"Order in the court", growls Judge Xkewsis as flash bulbs pop and reporters rush from the courtroom to file their stories. *"Ms. Payne does your client accept this offer?"*

"Yes your honor, if Ms. Writer will meet her deadlines and complete the novel." Ima nods her head.

"Ms. Writer, please stand." The judge shuffles his papers into a stack and announces his decision. *"This court accepts your plea of no contest to the charges of reckless procrastination. You are hereby*

sentenced to prepare an outline for your novel, to write daily, set a reasonable deadline for completion and to never set foot in my court again." The judge bangs his gavel. *"Case dismissed!"*

The chances of you doing a day in court for procrastination are slim. However, the case does illustrate how you can allow other tasks to get in the way of what you should be doing.

Embrace Your Plan

Your belief your plan will work is half the battle. Your schedule is not forced. It is set up so you can accomplish what you want to do. Your priorities are your freedom. You maintain energy and resist stress because you know what is coming. No guesswork or frustration. You look at any day and know what to expect.

Embrace your plan does not mean to rigidly adhere to your plan every second. That would be too mechanical. You can allow for flexibility and adapt your plan according to current events. Someone may have tickets to a ballgame or concert unexpectedly. Look at your plan and see where it can be rearranged. If so, then go for it. If not, stay on plan.

Review Plan

Look at your plans at the end of the week. Did you accomplish what you meant to? Are there areas that could use some tweaking? Go ahead and make the adjustments. It's your plan. It can be dynamic and evergreen. The biggest question is: "Does it work for you?" Sometimes ideas work in our heads and look nice on paper but just don't work out. That's okay – fix it. It's your plan make it work for you.

Reward Yourself

You have worked hard to get your time in order and manage it properly. When it works – Celebrate!! Reward yourself for a job well done.

You have the POWERR™ to manage your time wisely. Start today for time is on your side.

14

Health-Love it or lose it

Nutrition, exercise, and sleep are the components of healthy living. The simplest health plan in the world is eat less, exercise more, and get enough sleep. Healthy living is a lifestyle. A healthy life style like everything else in life takes commitment.

The citizens of the United States according to the United States Department of Agriculture are all are overweight. Servings and portions that were sufficient 20 years ago have been replaced by super sizing and jumbo sizing. I remember as a young man getting full on an 8 oz bottle of Coca-Cola. I used to be just getting started at 20 ounces. Fortunately I've changed my eating habits and a good old cold soda is a treat rather than the norm.

There are a lot of books written on how to eat better or how to cook healthy meals and what to or not to eat. My mother would devise our meals by color. With something red, green, yellow along with the customary glass of milk. A simple meal would be corn, tomatoes, collard grains, cornbread and fish. Thinking back makes my mouth water. I wrote this poem to describe those absolutely delicious meals.

Home Cookin'

Morning calls for a bowl of Cream of Wheat
A butter belly button poised afloat

In finely grained cane to make it taste all sweet
And some cold milk for whitewashing your throat
Lunch is the marriage of two types of spread
Peanut butter and Concord grape jelly
Commingled as one while bounded by bread
No finer fare in anyone's deli
Dinner is a rainbow of color to please
Black bass, red snapper, white bass and blue gill
Fresh greens, red beans, macaroni and cheese
A medley in a kaleidoscope meal
It does not matter if you're young or old
Meals made at home are worth their weight in gold

The following guidelines were developed jointly by the United States Department of Agriculture and the Department of Health and Human Services.

Eat a variety of foods to get the energy, protein,
vitamins, minerals, and fiber you need for good
health.

Focus on foods. A variety of foods-whether fresh, frozen and, canned, or dried-rather than fruit juice for most of your food choices. For a 2,000 calorie diet, you will need 2 cups of fruit each day (for example, one small banana, one large orange, and the one quarter cup of dried apricots or peaches). Vary your veggies. Eat more dark green veggies, such as broccoli, kale, and other dark leafy greens; orange veggies, such as carrots, sweet potatoes, pumpkin, and winter squash; and beans and peas, such as pinto beans, kidney beans, black beans, garbanzo beans, split peas, and lentils.

Balance the food to eat with physical activity-
maintain or improve your weight to reduce your
chances of having high blood pressure, heart
disease, a stroke, certain cancers, and most
common kinds of diabetes.

*Choose a diet with plenty of grain products,
vegetables and fruits which provide needed
vitamins, minerals, fiber and complex
carbohydrates and can help you lower your intake of fat.*

Make half your grains whole grains. Eat at least 3 ounces of whole grain cereals, breads, crackers, rice, or pasta every day. One ounce is about one slice of bread, 1 cup of breakfast cereal, or 1/2 cup of cooked rice or pasta. Look to see that grains such as wheat, rice, or corn are referred to as "whole" in the list of ingredients.

*Choose a diet low in fat, saturated fat, and
cholesterol to reduce your risk of heart attack and
certain types of cancer and to help you maintain a
healthy weight.*

Go lean with protein. Choose lean meats and poultry. Bake it, broil it, or grill it. And vary your protein choices-with more fish, beans, peas, nuts, and seeds. Get your calcium-rich foods. Get 3 cups of low-fat or fat-free milk-or an equivalent amount of low-fat yogurt end/or low-fat cheese (one and one-half ounces of cheese equals1 cup of milk)-every day. For kids aged 2 to 8, it is 2 cups of milk. If you do not or cannot consume milk, choose lactose-free milk products and/or calcium-fortified foods and beverages.

*Choose a diet moderate in sugars. A diet with a lot
of sugars has too many calories and too few
nutrients for most people and can contribute to
tooth decay.*

*Choose a diet moderate in salts and sodium to help
reduce your risk of high blood pressure.*

Know the limits on fats, salt, and sugars. Read the Nutrition Facts label on foods. Look for foods low in saturated fats and Trans fats. Choose and prepare foods and beverages with little salt (sodium) and/or added sugars (caloric-sweeteners).

> *If you drink alcoholic beverages, do so in*
> *moderation. Alcoholic beverages supply calories,*
> *but little or no nutrients. Drinking alcohol is also*
> *the cause of many health problems and accidents*
> *and can lead to addiction.*

I will add one more point. Most healthy eating plans I have read include drinking plenty of water. According to most plans, you should drink 8 eight-ounce glasses of water per day. The principle behind this, I understand, is to get your body used to regular hydration and your body will not store water from the foods you eat. Hence, you do not carry the dreaded water weight.

Moderation and balance is key in the dietary guidelines. The second dietary guideline mentions the balance between the food we eat and physical activity.

The President's Council on physical fitness and sports has developed guidelines for personal exercise programs. The web site is **www.fitness.gov/fitness.html.** An excellent booklet called Fitness Fundamentals outlines components of a complete exercise program. A work out according to Fitness Fundamentals should include cardio respiratory endurance, muscular strength, muscular endurance, and flexibility. Each work out should begin with a warm-up and end with a cool down. As a general rule, space your workouts throughout the week and avoid consecutive days of hard exercise. Before starting any exercise program always check with your doctor to ensure you are physically ready.

The National Sleep Foundation does an annual poll called *Sleep in America*. The 2001 poll found a majority of American adults (63%) do not get the recommended eight hours of sleep needed for good health, safety, and optimum performance. In fact, nearly one-third (31%) report sleeping less than seven hours each week, though many adults say they tried to sleep more on weekends. The 2001 poll was supported by the NSF's 2002 *Sleep in America* poll in finding today Americans average 6.9 hours of sleep on weeknights and 7.5 hours per night on weekends. The 2002 poll further reports: while many Americans enjoy the benefit of sufficient sleep, as many as 47 million adults may be putting themselves at risk for injury, health, and behavior problems because they are not meeting their minimum sleep needs to be fully alert the next day.

We all have active lives but our bodies need recharging. The nature and the amount of our sleep will determine how well we live and how productive we are. Here are twelve approaches to better sleep.

1. Exercise regularly.
2. Reduce caffeine close to bedtime.
3. Avoid alcohol close to bedtime.
4. Limit eating a few hours before bedtime
5. Sleep on comfortable pillows and mattress.
6. Dress comfortably for bed.
7. Keep regular hours for going to bed and waking
8. Use the bedroom for rest and pleasure, remove the television and office materials.
9. Avoid smoking near bedtime. (nicotine is a stimulant)
10. Release the stress of the day, think of your bedroom as a sanctuary of rest.
11. Let sleep happen, do not try to force yourself to sleep.
12. Get up if you are not sleepy, read a book or watch television until you become drowsy.

There is an old story of a rich man who was hospitalized and terminally ill. Every day he asked his nurse to prop him up. He would look out of the window and watch as people strolled by. One morning as he gazed out the window he heard complaints coming from the hallway. The elevators were not working. Someone was complaining about walking up the stairs. He rang the nurse's station. He then asked to speak to the person who was complaining about the elevators. A young man walked in who seemed barely in his twenties. The old man looked at him with sad eyes and whispered, "I have more money than I can spend therefore more than I need. I would give it all to be able to walk up the stairs".

We all may not be monetarily wealthy but we all can be physically healthy. Eat, sleep and exercise your way to better health. Start today!!

15

Pursuing Performance that Pays

We are all performers. Actors perform in movies, athletes in sporting events, while most of us perform our duties at work. We work to get paid. If we did not get paid, our work would be a hobby. Performance management, once considered the responsibility of supervisors, is your responsibility also. Setting and understanding expectations for work is a key ingredient in performance success.

However, the world of performance management has been sullied by the murky and often unexplained expectations of one party versus another. A lot of stress is caused by misunderstandings. You must understand your primary duties in order to get paid. Let's call this filling your cup. Filling your cup is carrying your primary duties through to completion. Business is willing to trade money for full cups or overflowing cups. The trade off from all accounts is a great deal!

I always define my primary duties with my supervisor. We put into writing what is required. Once I know what is required I can figure out how to exceed those requirements.

The following three examples show my primary duties when I was a tire sales person. This example can be adapted for any job.

Tire Salesman Primary Duties (PDs)

1) Sell tires
2) Open credit cards
3) Housekeeping
4) Operations

My manager told me if I did the above I would be doing my job-filling my cup. The next step was to add measurements so that I could tell whether I was doing a good job or not. One key to pursuing performance that pays is: knowing good performance when you see it. I had to recognize when I was doing a good job and not have to wait for my manager to tell me so.

The next chart shows primary duties and specific metrics.

Tire Salesman Primary Duties (PDs)	Specific Metrics (SMs)
1) Sell tires	Avg. 12 tires per day per month
2) Open credit cards	Avg. 1 per day per month
3) Housekeeping	Clean restrooms daily
4) Operations	File invoices daily

I now know specifically what I need to do. I can check my own progress without my manager. I know what it takes to fill my cup.

All I need to do is document the results of my specific metrics for my annual performance appraisal.

At this point my employer and I have a balanced relationship. I deliver and he pays. What a wonderful country. So, what if I want more money? What if I want an increase in my weekly pay? What duties do I need to accomplish to earn more money?

My employer and I agreed that if I did the above I earned my weekly paycheck. However, according to my supervisor, if I exceeded my specific metrics I could be eligible for a pay increase. My ability to fill my cup until it overflows can get me more money. My actual performance looked like this.

Tire Salesman
Primary Duties (PDs)

1) Sell tires
2) Open credit cards
3) Housekeeping
4) Operations

Specific Metrics (SMs)	Results
Avg. 12 tires per day per month	16 tires per day
Avg. 1 per day per month	1.5 per day
Clean restrooms daily	Yes
File invoices daily	Yes

Documentation is vital for performance management. I developed a check sheet for restrooms and a daily sign off sheet for my invoices. I also kept my monthly results on tires and credit cards. I was prepared to have a factual discussion of my performance. It worked! I received a nice merit increase.

What if my performance results looked like this?

Specific Metrics (SMs)		Results
1)	Avg. 12 tires per day per month	10 tires per day
2)	Avg. 1 per day per month	0.8 per day
3)	Clean restrooms daily	No
4)	File invoices daily	Yes

Those results create a totally different conversation. It may not be pleasant but, it is not unexpected. That is the grace of defining primary duties and specific metrics ahead of time. There are no surprises when it is performance appraisal time. Pursuing performance that pays is successful when expectations are agreed upon and delivered.

Performance is everything. High-potential sometimes is valued over high-performance. High potential however is a promise while high-performance is delivery and more. High-potential may open the door but high-performance gets you in the house.

16

Assess Your Assets

Make the most of yourself; for that is all there is of you.
Ralph Waldo Emerson

Assets are generally thought of in financial terms. Net worth, how many cars you own or investments in stocks and bonds are considered assets. These are important but you have more assets. You have personal qualities and traits that are your assets. Some assets come so naturally they are not often recognized: the ability to make people laugh, organizational skills, cooking, foreign languages, math, nurturing, and more.

My basic three are: protect your good name, your ability to communicate and common sense.

Protect your good name.

One's good name is a theme that is played out in many movies and stories. The hero has been mistakenly accused of wrongdoing. He goes to any length to clear his name. Like the movies reputation, plays a big part in how we are perceived and treated.

I've seen people embraced because someone knew a parent or grandparent. Many times I've heard comments like this:

"Let him in, that's Mabel's boy"
"He's okay. He's a McKenzie."
'You're Big Man's son? Come on in."

A reputation is a hindrance if it is negative. Goodwill becomes ill will if you become known for unethical and questionable behavior. Honor and integrity are ingredients of a good reputation. A good reputation protects your good name. Protect your good name and you'll have one asset that no one can take from you.

Ability to communicate.

You must be heard. You must be able to get your ideas understood. The ability to communicate is crucial in a fast paced world. There is situational communication. We speak differently depending on circumstances. There's business communication, public social communication, private social communication, family communication and a multitude of communication combining, subtracting and adding to the above.

As a boy growing up in the South, my mother admonished me to speak the "King's English". That was a way of telling me to speak clearly and precisely. It was a common practice in our family to be corrected mid-sentence and have to repeat whatever we were saying correctly. I catch myself doing that as an adult and my wife tells me it is annoying. My mother was preparing me to compete outside of my community, where how one speaks is a calling card.

Communication runs in cycles. Growing up, we were coached on speaking proper English. There was however, always the hip talk of the street, the words and slang in a code that those in crowd understood but misunderstood by the mainstream. It was labeled as counterculture-but cool. I picked up that slang and spoke that way with my friends and could switch when necessary. The key is the flexibility of being heard and understood by those who need to hear and understand. Now hip-hop is the counter culture street language that interestingly has invaded mainstream America.

Do you know how you sound or how others hear you? Listening to your recorded voice is a good way to improve diction and voice quality. Record your voice and play it back. You hear your voice internally and it is not the same as how others hear you. Before I speak to a group, I record my speech. It is a great way to check for understanding and clarity.

The ability to communicate means people understand you. That's the bottom line. Understanding and mastering your ability to communicate will aid in your success. You must be heard.

Common Sense

Give yourself credit for having common sense. Some things you just know and they fit in. Technically common sense is the ability to think in terms congruent to societal norms. (Now that's a mouthful) Described like that, it may not seem to be a great thing but it is. There are times that we must connect with the world outside ourselves on its terms.

Common sense has grown from everyday occurrences that people share. Common sense is wisdom from grandparents and parents and the neighborhood. Warnings from Miss Holly, the librarian, or stories from Mr. Johnson at the barbershop yield common sense. Anytime you hear a sentence begin with, - "Everyone knows that …" someone is about to lay some wisdom on you.

Everyone knows that:

If your barber stops talking and starts whistling he has messed up your haircut.

If you mix colors and whites in the wash it's a disaster.

If you step into oncoming traffic you're going to get hit.

Russell L Drake

If you grab a cast iron skillet by the handle without an oven mitt you will get burned.

One girl rabbit and one boy rabbit... you get the picture.

Personal Asset Inventory System

I have developed a Personal Asset Inventory System (PAIS) guide to document your assets. The PAIS is divided into three sections: technical, social and academic. The document is fluid in that it can be updated at any time.

Technical Assets
　　Work experiences -current and past
　　Military
　　Product Knowledge
　　Industry experience
　　Vocational skills
　　Other

Social Assets
　　Language skills
　　Professional memberships, licenses, certifications
　　International experiences
　　Fraternal/Social memberships
　　Charitable/Volunteering
　　Personal achievements
　　Life skills
　　Other

Academic Assets
　　Levels of education
　　Degrees in progress
　　School of Hard Knocks
　　Life experiences

The PAIS will change as you grow and gain experiences. Update it as needed and refer to it as a reminder of your valuable assets. You are an inventory of all there is of you and now you can write it down and share it if you wish.

17

Study the Areldee Window

Awareness of what is…a snapshot in time…a glimpse of life in a microcosm…a look at an event from outside the event. That is the rationale behind the 𝕬𝖗𝖊𝖑𝖉𝖊𝖊 𝖂𝖎𝖓𝖉𝖔𝖜.

Our lives are divided among four windows:

Physical	Spiritual
Social	Technical

These four windows in different combinations cover our activities, dreams, hopes, desires, work, failures, successes essentially everything.

What does the windows mean in the 𝕬𝖗𝖊𝖑𝖉𝖊𝖊 𝖂𝖎𝖓𝖉𝖔𝖜?

Physical

Physical is matter that is perceived by one or more senses or material things of substance, experience, or environment. We are generally given the ability to see, hear, touch, taste and smell our environment. Physical is reception. The physical world exists because we exist and are able to receive it through our senses.

There is an age old question. If a tree falls in the woods and no one is there to hear it, does it make a sound? Usually people smile and remark how deep the question is but never give an answer.

Does sound exist outside of us? Sound is a sensation stimulated in the organs of hearing by a vibratory disturbance. Our five senses are receptors that connect us to the physical world.

How would you answer the question if it were phrased like this? If a tree's falling creates a vibratory disturbance and there were no organs of hearing to stimulate would there be sound?

What do you think?

The physical world of course is so much more: The beauty of a sunset, the smell of wild flowers, the taste of your favorite foods, and the wind against your face or the melodious beat of summer rain on roof tops.

In the 𝕬𝖗𝖊𝖑𝖉𝖊𝖊 𝖂𝖎𝖓𝖉𝖔𝖜, the physical is where the world and you intersect.

Spiritual

Spiritual is from the Latin word *spiritus* meaning inspiration or breathe of God. One's spirit connects with emotions through a range of feelings that rise independently rather than through conscious effort. Feelings like love, sadness, reverence, apathy, or joy.

Inspiration can be found around us or in us. Inspiration occurs when we acknowledge the majesty of our physical world or the unlimited opportunities granted by our Creator.

The breath of God signifies life. James Weldon Johnson used the theme as a poetic element in his poem, *The Creation*. In the poem he described God scooping up a lump of clay and shaping it in His own image:

> *"Then into it he blew the breath of life,*
> *And man became a living soul. Amen. Amen."*

In the 𝕬𝖗𝖊𝖑𝖉𝖊𝖊 𝖂𝖎𝖓𝖉𝖔𝖜, ones' spirit can be seen as an essential and activating principle.

Social

Social is having or experiencing something with others. We share our experiences with our family, friends, partners and others.

Our human instinct is to band together with others who share our common interests. That explains the many different types of social organizations that exist.

Churches, choirs, ensembles, fraternities, lodges, athletic teams, bridge clubs, poker night, quilting bees, cheerleaders, book clubs, bird watchers, democrats, republicans, socialists, libertarians, green party, religious right, conservatives, liberals, agnostics, atheists, gangs, guilds, unions, communists, pacifists, right-to-lifers, orchestras, school bands, societies, haves, have nots, rich, poor, boy bands, girl bands, rock bands, pop bands, jazz bands, hip hop, heavy metal, pen pals, dance teams, honor societies and more.

In the Arelbee Window, our social needs are fulfilled from our association and involvement with people who share our interests.

Technical

Technical is comprised of fraternal twins – art and skill. Art is the high quality conception found in works of beauty.

Skill is expertness. One shows the ability, dexterity and proficiency to execute techniques or systems that require the use of one's body or hands.

Technical can sometimes be seen as a hybrid. Technical pulls in aspects from physical and spiritual to create art or execute techniques that build bridges or assemble a bicycle.

Growing up I heard the adults in my family talk about folks that had "a way with" something. Mr. Price has a way with wood. He can take lumber and turn it into fine furniture. Mrs. Royster has a way with a garden. She has the best tomatoes on the block. Little Jimmy has a way with tools. He can fix anything.

The people mentioned above all had technical abilities to build, grow, or fix things that amazed others.

In the 𝔄𝔯𝔢𝔩𝔡𝔢𝔢 𝔚𝔦𝔫𝔡𝔬𝔴, the technical window is sometimes hidden but is available to all of us.

One can use the 𝔄𝔯𝔢𝔩𝔡𝔢𝔢𝔚𝔦𝔫𝔡𝔬𝔴 to appraise and enjoy an event. Take Thanksgiving dinner:

Physical – We see our relatives, we hug and kiss, we hear the great stories, we smell the aroma of the feast, and we taste the holiday libations and meal.

Spiritual - The emotional smorgasbord that comes with family and friends gathering inspires our lives.

Social – Family and friends are gathered for a shared experience of comfort and food.

Technical – The expert hands craft the culinary fare that delights the eye, warms the soul and fills the tummy!

Awareness of what is…a snapshot in time…a glimpse of life in a microcosm…a look at an event from outside the event. This is the 𝔄𝔯𝔢𝔩𝔡𝔢𝔢 𝔚𝔦𝔫𝔡𝔬𝔴.

18

Self-Affirmations

I am often inspired by the words of others. Quotes from famous and not so famous people have served as inspiration for this book and other endeavors in my life. I feel energized when the right words capture my sentiments and clarify my understanding of an idea. The thoughts and ideas of others are powerful and so are one's own thoughts and ideas.

An affirmation is a positive true statement. Self-affirmations are positive true statements about you. What can be more wonderful than to say something positive and true about who you are? One step further is to say something positive and true about who you can become. Self-talk is motivation customized specifically for you by you. You are your own counselor and cheerleader.

Rev. Jesse Jackson, founder of the Rainbow Coalition, shared an affirmation that millions grew to love and believe. "I am somebody". Simple words loaded with meaning for a disenfranchised people. The wonderful part of this affirmation is that anyone, regardless of race, sex, or political affirmation can declare it and it is true.

"I am somebody" is a true positive statement.

I started using self-affirmations a few years after college. I was unfocused and undisciplined in completing projects and I needed a talking too. So, I decided to talk to myself. I developed a series of self-affirmations to sharpen my attitude. One area that I had to address was staying up late watching Johnny Carson or a movie. Naturally my eyes were drooping in the morning and I felt sluggish the first few hours at work. I needed some sleep!!

****

Self-affirmation # 1
I go to bed at a reasonable time so that I get seven hours sleep, wake up rested and ready to start my day.

****

I had a friend who enjoyed long distance running and we ran together four days a week. Long distance running always picks me up. A runner's high is fantastic. After our run, we would cool down with a casual jog and talk. The conversation would start off an easy conversation but always ended up about his divorce. No matter what we began talking about, we always end up talking about his former marriage. I would then join in with whatever negative issue I had going on in my life. My energy and elation from the run would dissipate and the effects of the run would disappear. It took a while for me to recognize the situation. Unfortunately, after telling my running buddy I would no longer discuss or listen to stories about his former marriage we stopped running together. I missed running with him but I did not miss the issues.

****

Self-affirmation #2
I surround myself with people who have a positive energy and do not to dwell on negative issues.

****

I am a pack rat. I collect used-to-mean-something-but-I-have-forgotten-what-it-was-for-stuff. I also, through some unnatural gene live by the philosophy, "it will get done when it needs to get done". Of course, that philosophy was not going to work in the business world. I needed to be organized and timely in my work. This affirmation was a statement of what I wanted to be. It was not accomplished immediately. I knew that it would surface if I kept reminding myself on a daily basis.

****

Self-affirmation #3
I am organized. I prioritize my work and pursue each item until completed.

****

Staying in shape and in eating properly is a personal value. I ran cross country, played basketball, studied martial arts, ballroom dancing, and embraced golf!! I've been a meat eater and a vegetarian on many different levels. I understand that dieting is a temporary nutrition plan. One must think in terms of a lifestyle change when it comes to how one eats. Also, it takes a behavior change to incorporate an exercise plan that makes sense and is fun.

****

Self-affirmation #4
I live a healthy lifestyle by eating properly and exercising to keep physically fit.

****

I have been fortunate to have had the support of a good family. My parents and grandparents, uncles and aunts created a loving environment that I've worked hard to perpetuate. The next affirmation grew as my personal situation changed with marriage and children.

****

Self-affirmation #5
I am the best son, brother, husband, father, grandfather I can be. My family is important and I care, support and love them unconditionally.

****

My affirmations have grown over the years. The five you have read are my priorities right now. Your list will develop and expand as the possibilities in your life develop and expand.

Self-affirmations are reinforcement of who you are or who you want to be. Write your affirmations on index cards and read them out loud. There is power in your speech. Read them out loud at least three times a day. Read them in the morning when you wake, at midday when working or at home, and once before you go asleep. The morning reading helps you jump-start your day. The mid-day reading helps reinforce these positive feelings you have for yourself. The evening reading prepares your subconscious for a restful sleep and once again reinforces who you are and who you strive to be. You are your own inspiration.

19

Isolate 15 minutes a day

This technique has worked well for me in writing. Years ago when I wanted to publish my poetry, I needed a method to make it happen. I generally wrote when the mood hit me. If I was in a creative mood I might turn out a couple of poems a week. Then I might not write for a while. As long as I was writing for my personal satisfaction, it did not matter how long I took. One day the possibility of being a published poet revealed itself in the form of a friend.

I was attending a national conclave for my fraternity, Phi Beta Sigma, one summer. My friend and fraternity brother Tyrone Parnell was setting up as a vendor in the retail marketplace. Tyrone was setting up his booth to sell his book of poetry. I was surprised and excited! We talked about how he got published and he offered to help me do the same. At that moment I knew that I needed discipline in order to create enough poetry to publish my own book.

The hit or miss approach to writing was not going to work now. I had to be consistent in my approach. I decided to isolate fifteen minutes a day for writing. Fifteen minutes did not seem like a lot of time to set aside considering I still had a job, grass to cut, and other family matters to handle.

So I sat down with my pen and paper and began my journey to publish my first book of poetry. The most wonderful thing happened. I realized after a few days that I was writing for more than 15 minutes. I designated my 15 minutes to start at 9:00 PM. That gave me plenty of time after work to eat, read the paper and talk to my wife.

There were times that I would sit at the kitchen table and just hold my pen waiting for anything to come. Most of the times a thought or phrase would surface and off I would go creating the poetry to match my thoughts. Some days were used for editing and rewriting but always something was being accomplished. My writing time expanded. I would write for more than 15 minutes a day. Let me clarify when I say writing for more than 15 minutes. If I could write constantly for that long it would be amazing for me. A part of the time was thinking and trying verses and thinking and trying different techniques. It was a time of exploring and creativity. When it was all said and done I had written enough poetry to publish my first book, *"A Walk in the Park"*. What a personal triumph!! I tip my hat to Tyrone for the inspiration. I used the same method of isolating 15 minutes a day for my second book, *"The Sounds of Truth"* and my jazz spoken word compact disc, *"When I Think of You"*.

The principle behind isolating 15 minutes a day is taking baby steps. We can be overwhelmed by our routine and do not do the things we want to do. Or, if we take time out, we feel guilty that we are letting something else slide. That is why we start with 15 minutes a day. There are 1440 minutes in a 24-hour day. What's 15 minutes? Not much in the scheme of things. One way to monitor your time initially is to designate a time to start and to stop. Next set the timer on the microwave or stove or alarm clock for 15 minutes. When the alarm or beeper goes off, your time is up. You are done. You will have completed your fifteen minutes and accomplished your goal that day.

It does not matter the activity. You can isolate time for any activity. My activity was writing. Your activity could be reading, walking, or restoring a piece of furniture. It does not matter. It is your time. I set aside my time at 9:00 p.m. and made sure nothing will interfere with that time. My wife was gracious not to engage me at that time. I did not take phone calls or otherwise miss my fifteen minutes. I was surprised how much television I was willing to give up. I've used this technique for writing this book. I think in terms of setting aside an hour for writing. Sometimes, I must admit, the words just do not flow. I do not get up and leave. I will sit there skim through the dictionary or go over what I've written on previous days. My discipline is sticking with my time. I never know when an idea could surface. Heaven forbid if I am not there, I might miss that one idea that will make a difference!

It is possible to isolate fifteen minutes a day for different activities. One example is when I wanted to paint my rooms upstairs. Instead of tackling the job of taping all at once, I did it in fifteen minute segments over a couple of days. It works for me and it can work for you. Try it yourself. Take whatever activity interests you and dedicate fifteen minutes a day. Try it for five days. You will be five days closer to your goal and you will become more passionate than ever.

20

Overcoming Obstacles

A sage writer wrote, "When we remove the greatest obstacle to success-ourselves, we can do anything." It is an interesting idea that we get in our own way more than any other thing or person. We set limitations and rules that prevent us from moving forward, these self-imposed restrictions limit our creativity and ability to solve problems within our control.

How often have you heard "I can't do this or no way it's impossible?" Self-defeating comments are based on our own perception of the problem, not others. There may have been instances in the past when you did not accomplish what you wanted. A setback may have ingrained in your psyche that you cannot do the task at all. That does not preclude you from doing it in the future. It only means you could not do it in the past.

When I first learned how to play basketball, I was not very tall. I remember eating a lot of rubber from having my shot blocked back into my face.

We played a game called 21. Each player played for himself. If you made a basket, you got to shoot free throws. You could shoot up to three free throws as long as you made them consecutively. When a player scored seven points, all players without any points had to move to the sideline and watch. There were many days I had to sit out at seven. Sometimes I would luck in a shot but still be eliminated at eleven. Players with two points or less had to sit out at eleven. I realized that if I was going to overcome being on the sideline, I was going to have to make my free throws. I started practicing free throws every day. It took a while, but when I made a basket I made my free throws. Those three free throws gave me five points and that kept me in the game. Now my confidence at that point was high and with a little luck and practice I was the guy sending players to the sidelines at seven and eleven.

I led all the teams I played for (high school, college, and industrial leagues) in free-throw shooting. Over the years, I have been known to win a free-throw shooting contest or two.

All obstacles are not self-imposed. There are forces in the world that inadvertently or purposely put obstacles before us. So what should we do? My suggestion is to ICE ^{2} them.

IDENTIFY, CLARIFY, ERASE, or EMBRACE

Identify – determine what the obstacle is and any defining characteristics. What is the obstacle/problem/challenge? The idea here is to look at the problem objectively. What is it? What is its shape? How does it feel? What does this have to do with me? Where does it come from?

If you are in the dark, and you stumble you may turn on a light. Identify is the metaphoric "turn on the light phase".

Clarify – understand the obstacle and view it clearly. Seek understanding. Where does the obstacle originate? Why is it here? What elements help me make sense of this issue? Who has a similar issue that can help me?

Erase or Embrace – remove all traces of the obstacle, submit with dignity or exercise your power over it with vigor and determination. Some obstacles disappear when approached from a different perspective. Others stay as part of our personal landscape and are used to make us stronger or better.

James Earl Jones has one of the most recognizable and authoritative voices on the planet. Did you know that he barely spoke as a child? He hid in muteness and embarrassment because of his stuttering.

Lance Armstrong overcame testicular cancer to win seven consecutive Tour de France cycling titles.

Wilma Rudolph overcame polio to become an Olympic gold medalist.

Ray Charles and Stevie Wonder, critically acclaimed blind musicians, are universally known for their talent and contributions to music and the world.

They all used some form of ICE^2 to rise to the level of success they enjoyed. The first two steps, identify and clarify our universal. Erase or embrace are the wild cards.

Mr. Jones, Mr. Armstrong and Ms. Rudolph were able to erase their challenges. Mr. Charles and Mr. Wonder embraced their challenges.

The spark that ignites the flame of possibility and furnishes the power to overcome obstacles is within all of us. The essence of truth universal to all of us is – we are always right. If we say we are able or not able to overcome an obstacle, we are right.

"Adversity builds character"
Me.

A life lesson for my children has been my adversity quote. We do not find out who we are until we are tested. It is easy to profess love and kindness when all is well. Only when adversity or an obstacle is placed before you, does your character and resolve surface.

I am an avid golfer. A golf course is a magical place filled with adventure and intrigue. The panoramic view of trees, lakes and sand traps create a panoramic view that is breathtaking and beautiful.

Your perspective changes, however, if you leave the fairway and roll behind a tree, land in a sand trap or splash into a lake. It has been often said that you can find out who a person is by their demeanor on the golf course. Is the golfer calm? What does the golfer do to get back on course? How does the golfer handle adversity?

A pearl is a valuable jewel but where does it come from? To the oyster a grain of sand is an irritant that can't be scratched.

The oyster embraces the irritant by secreting a crystalline substance called pearl nacre. Layers upon layers are added until the irritant no longer exists. The result is comfort for the oyster and a valued commodity in a jewelry market. In this case, if there were no obstacle there would be no challenge and no pearl.

The following is a hierarchy from the American Heritage Dictionary of English Language that I call the Chart of Challenges:

Obstacle – applies broadly to that which must be removed, circumvented or surmounted.

Obstruction – strongly suggests physical interference with passage.

Bar/barrier – stresses difficulty of passage to the point of implying prohibition, exclusion or confinement.

Block – suggests equally strong opposition of more temporary duration.

Impediment – implies interference with normal functions, but no end of function.

Hindrance – implies a mere delay.

Encumbrance – implies something that weighs you down like clutter.

Snag – something which provides unforeseen, and usually brief or short lived opposition.

You control your destiny. A person that is calm under pressure is characterized as cool. So whenever you need to overcome obstacles – "Just ICE [2] them".

21

Networking

Networking is building alliances that are helpful to you and others. You should carefully prepare yourself when you start a network. The purpose is to have resources at your disposal when needed. Alliances are created by preparation and purpose. Networking is a way of reaching out to others to advance your agenda or the agenda of others.

Networking can start anywhere. You can start with relatives, friends or recommendations from others. Your network should include a doctor, lawyer, real estate agent and possibly the chief of police.

I have moved many times throughout the Midwest, South, and East Coast. My first contact in a new place is a real estate agent. My real estate agent has been valuable in helping me start a network in new places. The real estate agent knows the nearest hospital, grocery stores and services in my new area. I have often made contacts through my real estate agent. I introduce myself to the people at the bank and cleaners when I move into a new community. Most people are open to new residents and they have welcomed my family and me with open arms. The local community center or YW/MCA has programming that helps you meet people and develop your network.

Contact with folks who have the potential to become a part of your network comes with conversation and a genuine interest in others. You can't be like a salesman who "cards" everyone he meets. You have to take time to inquire, listen and reflect on what is being said. An authentic interest in others is the quickest way to develop a network.

Networking has to be balanced. In other words it has to work for you and those in your network. They must receive a benefit from knowing you as well as you knowing them. Networking alliances are created when your skills and talents connect with the needs of others or vice-versa

Let's discuss network preparation. There is an old saying, "The time to repair the roof is when the sun shines." A raging storm would not be the time to climb on the roof to make repairs. My grandmother when preparing a Sunday meal would take out a chicken to thaw long before it was time to cook. One must be prepared when an event takes place.

You are your own first impression. How do you look? How do you greet others? How do you gather information and share information? Networking is effective when both parties feel there is something to gain. Networking is not getting to know people so that you can use them later. One sided transactions will destroy any healthy alliances.

Personal appearance is important. Now is the time for us to remember all the things we learned from our parents. You should have a neat appearance, polished shoes, a steady handshake and a smile. That's a start.

A small notepad and pen are valuable networking tools. Many people do not carry a business card so you have to be prepared to write down any information available. You must be discrete. If you are scribbling notes as you are talking to people they may become suspicious. They may find you suspicious. Be prepared to talk about yourself. After all, you want others to learn who you are. An important step in networking is follow up. A short note after meeting someone shows that you are interested and wish to establish an open line of communication or relationship.

A simple method is to file any business cards you have gathered for future reference. Current technology supports scanning business cards to a file so the information is available on your desktop or laptop computer. Either way, you have the information stored.

One can keep ones' network current by following up periodically. A quick call, e-mail or a highlighted article of interest can keep your network fresh.

For some people the fear of networking comes right after public speaking. If you follow this formula you can get started with ease.

I call it IL to the second power. Introduce. Listen. Inquire. Listen. Here is a script.

Introduce: Hello, I am (your name).
Listen: (they most likely will introduce themselves)
Inquire: I am new to (the organization). What do you like best about (the organization)?
Listen. Listen. Listen.

I wish I could say that all networking is productive. Some are not. You should move on if the conversation becomes frivolous or the person you speak to is non-responsive. It happens sometimes. You just move on.

You should decide what your objectives are for the evening. Are you trying to make business contacts, social contacts or both? If you are making business contacts you should research the organization before you get there. Set a goal for how many contacts you want to make that evening, take action and make it happen.

The same approach is used for social gatherings. For example: You are invited to the Kiwanis Club Annual Charity Ball. You should research the event. Especially understand who benefits from the charity. Armed with your information, you are prepared for the event. A donation also goes a long way to starting your network within the organization.

Networking is enhanced when you share it with your spouse. Always disclose your plans and reward your spouse when he/she helps you.

You can expand your network by sharing Other Peoples Network. If you have ten contacts in your network and they each have ten contacts you can expand to one hundred contacts. The expansion can compound exponentially if the sharing is acceptable and authentic.

There are no boundaries in networking. An authentic smile, eye contact and a friendly handshake will advance many opportunities. Your new network will expand your horizons and create an interaction of give and take. The more you have to offer the greater your network.

22

Avoid Attitude Misunderstandings

Attitude can sometimes be a misunderstood word. One reason is based on its context; the word could reflect good behavior or bad behavior.

Attitude defined by itself, usually means someone with a problem. "He has an attitude." "She thinks she's something with that attitude." People are judged, tried and hung by what is perceived as a bad attitude.

So what? Why should we care? Well, in some cases, we should not. But overall, we need to be aware of our behavior known as attitude.

Perception of who we are is seen as a window into a personality. It is interesting that when a person is perceived to have the right behavior, the word attitude is modified. He has the right attitude. She has a positive attitude. This concept has affected many jobs, relationships, because of individual definitions of attitude.

My take is attitude is a learned behavior. You can learn to have a positive or negative attitude.

It is interesting that many people don't see how their attitude affects people around them. Their attitude can be judged by the behavior of folks around them. The reaction or actions of those around you can bring clarity to your attitude. Keep in mind that sometimes people's perception of you may be unfair, and simply wrong. However, consider the following questions when you think about your attitude. Do people want to be around you? Does your boss compliment your work? When you discuss subjects with friends - are they defensive or open?

Let's use the 𝕬𝖗𝖊𝖑𝖉𝖊𝖊𝖂𝖎𝖓𝖉𝖔𝖜 (Chapter 17) to view attitude.

𝕻hysical attitude is non-verbal communication. It is a combination of facial expressions, posture, and gestures. These signals can unconsciously communicate our mood. These signals are picked up by the people around us. How can non-verbal communication translate or be interpreted as a positive attitude?

Facial expressions
  – Consistent eye contact
  – smiling relaxed face
Posture
  – Body relaxed
  – turns to person speaking
  – Brisk, erect walk
Gestures
  – Open palms
  – Hands movement unrestrained

How can body language translate or be interpreted as a negative attitude?

Facial expressions
  – Lips are pursed
  – Intense eye contact
Posture
  – fidgeting.
  – leaning away creating space.
Gestures
  – Arms tense, with hands balled into fists
  – Arms crossed

A person's body language may not represent their true emotional state or tell the whole story. The above are possibilities but, a frown may be from a headache. Arms crossed may mean a person is cold. As we peer through the 𝕬𝖗𝖊𝖑𝖉𝖊𝖊 𝖂𝖎𝖓𝖉𝖔𝖜 we can see how non-verbal communication (physical) can be perceived by others.

Spiritual attitude is a state of mind or an activating principle of a person. A positive attitude does not mean a Pollyanna view of life through rose colored glasses. A positive attitude reflects hope and determination; our openness to explore the myriad of possibilities in life that points us toward our goals. A positive attitude is a strong spirit that excites us, stirs up our juices and consciously moves us forward.

𝕬 negative attitude doesn't do that. To say it is the opposite is too simple. A negative attitude is debilitating. It is a pessimistic glass half empty approach to life that creates barriers. It clouds your vision of possibilities, and inhibits your progress. You have a choice, why not be positive?

Social attitude connects with others. When we interact with people, our attitude can affect them. Like a beacon that guides ships in safely on a foggy night, a positive attitude can light the way for others.

Technical attitude represents a set of skills. You can develop these skills by consciously practicing the best of a physical, spiritual and social attitude: non-verbal communication that is open, a spirit that is motivating, and a willingness to share with others.

23

Negotiate Your Outcomes

Everything is negotiable if you choose to negotiate. There are many options in life available if we're willing to give a little in order to get what we want. Effective negotiation is a combination of knowledge, understanding time frames, and being able to make the deal.

Negotiation is often thought of in business terms. Management versus workers. Benefit maintenance versus cutbacks. The haves versus the have-nots. Negotiation is everywhere.

Who are the best negotiators in the world? Would it surprise you to find out the best negotiators don't even know how to speak? The answer is babies. Think about it. When a baby needs or wants something, the crying starts. When the baby is satisfied, the crying stops. End of negotiation. Some may think the negotiation is one-sided, but it depends on your perspective.

Three factors in negotiation are information, time, and power. Information is doing your research or due diligence. Time is understanding the period designated for the negotiation. Power is the authority to get things done.

There are three types of negotiations: Win-Win, Win-Lose and Lose-Lose. The first is the best type and the last is the worst.

Win – Win

This negotiation ends in a mutually acceptable agreement. Both parties are satisfied with the result. The give-and-take process has been used and both parties can claim victory.

Win – Lose

To the victor go the spoils. This negotiation has a party that "takes home all the marbles". The other party gets nothing. This may work for you if you're the winner, if this is a one-time deal, if you never see the party again, if the win doesn't damage your reputation. Those are a lot of ifs. The loser is disappointed but has to move on. But, the loser will never forget and somehow, somewhere, someone will pay for that loss.

Lose – Lose

This is the ultimate in ineffective negotiations. Both parties are unwilling to explore a mutually accepted agreement. Both parties are denied the benefits of an agreement. Both parties subscribe to the misery loves company theory or if I can't have it neither can you. This is not a good negotiating end and is a waste of time and effort.

Earlier I mentioned babies are great negotiators. Which type of negotiation do you think happens between parent and child? I see it as a win-win negotiation. A mother's desire is to nurture and keep her baby safe. A baby's cry is a signal that he or she needs something. The mother gives the baby, what it wants. Two needs are served. The baby is full or its diapers are dry, and the mother's need to nurture and protect is satisfied.

What about going shopping to make a purchase?

The most positive and practical of the three types of negotiation is Win – Win. You should pursue this type with persistence and determination.

My wife and I went to a furniture closeout sale. We browsed among the many items available and settled on a leather couch with a matching loveseat. We had shopped around and felt the price of the set was reasonable. On the spot, we decided to buy. In major buying negotiations, my wife is my go-between. She and I whisper to each other, and she presents the offer. We go back and forth until we reach an agreement. Sometimes I will open up an account with the store. I do not pay interest. I will pay the card off immediately. I'm just drawing the salesman into the negotiation. When my account is approved, the salesman knows I can afford the purchase, if I choose to buy.

On this day, we open an account and then tell the salesman to write up the sale. He's licking his chops because he can see a commission coming his way. The salesman starts to review the sale price, the tax and the delivery charge. Delivery charge? I tell him I don't want pay a delivery charge. He explains to me that the delivery person is an outside contractor and must be paid. I told him with the cost of the furniture over $4000, I would not pay a delivery charge. He told me he could not waive the feet. I told him I was not buying the furniture. I turned and walked away. My wife turned with me, and as we walked away she asked me, "What's wrong with you?" It's a good deal. Are you going to throw it away for $40? I quieted her as we walked and told her to walk slowly but steadily to the door. Just as I reached to open the door, the salesman called to me across the room. He had "talked to his manager" and waived the delivery charge.

What happened? I used information, time, and my power. I had shopped other stores and knew the price on the furniture was a real close out price. That was my information. The store was selling their shelves and fixtures. So I knew time was a factor. The salesman had a live customer and his own commission on the line. He had to consider the cost of the delivery, versus his lost commission. Time was a factor for him. The last piece was I had the power to walk away from the deal.

In this scenario, the salesman was bargaining with furniture. I was bargaining with money. In the end we both won. I got the furniture, and he got my money. WIN-WIN!!

Everything is negotiable. So, negotiate!!

24

Deconstructing the Twelve Inch Rule

June 1, 1980 was a wondrous day for me. I was inducted into the glorious band of Phi Beta Sigma fraternity, Inc. on the campus of Kentucky State University. The ceremony was solemn and serious, uplifting and passionate, symbolic and powerful. While pledging I learned a lesson that all men of Phi Beta Sigma fraternity learned. It is called the Twelve Inch rule. These are 12 instructions that represent a way of life.

Time Value

"To everything there is a season and time to every purpose under the heavens." Ecclesiastes 3:1

There is a time for any and everything you want to do. Lesson 13 was about taking control of time. Time value is an appreciation of time. You can measure time. You can tell someone the hours and minutes of the day. You can measure how fast a person runs a race or how long it takes to drive to work. These are objective facts depending on the accuracy of your watch or of your cell phone. You can review historical events, ponder current activities, or daydream about future events.

Time value is the place and order of things. How long does it take to fasten a seatbelt? The value of fastening your seatbelt grows exponentially if you are in an accident.

Time value is living in and an appreciation of the moments in life that makes life worth living. Consider: A child's first step; your first kiss; a home cooked meal or the moment you fell in love.

Time value is being cognizant of the past but not left in the past; knowing and appreciating what is happening now but still able to look to the future.

Best Performance of Duty

There is a story about student preparing a term paper. The student took the paper to his professor for some early feedback. The professor looked at one page and said, "You can do better".

The student revised the paper and returned it to the professor. The professor glanced at the paper and said once again, "You can do better".

The student reworked the paper two more times with the same comment from the professor. Finally, the student exclaimed, "I can't change this anymore. I have done the best I can." That is when the professor relented and said, "Now I will read your paper".

The lesson here is:

Be relentless in your task and do your best the first time.

Perseverance

Continue under all circumstances. Pursue your objectives with dogged determination. We all know the story of the tortoise and the hare. The rabbit was very talented and blessed with speed. The tortoise was blessed with the indomitable spirit of perseverance. While the rabbit showed off and mocked the tortoise, the tortoise slowly moved forward. While the rabbit ran circles around the tortoise, the tortoise continuously moved forward. In the end the rabbit grew weary and the tortoise won the race.

*"It does not matter how slowly you go, so long
as you do not stop."*   Confucius

The Worth of Example

Everyone needs a role model. There is power in what we project and do. I can remember as a child wanting to be like my Father. He was a military man. He was well groomed, punctual and proud. I was proud of him and proud to be his son.

Set a good example. You never know who may be watching.

The Virtue of Patience

No matter how we wish that some events would speed up, they take time. There is an old saying – "Good things come to those that wait." Assuming that is true, waiting is a good enough reason to be patient. Patience will allow events to unfold naturally. Patience can save us from embarrassment and misunderstanding while uncovering particulars of which we may not have been aware.

Talent Expression

"Our deepest fear is not that we aren't adequate. Our deepest fear is that we are powerful beyond measure. It is our light, not our darkness, that most frightens us. We ask ourselves, who am I to be brilliant, gorgeous, talented, and fabulous? Actually who are you not to be? You are a child of God; your playing small doesn't serve the world. There is nothing enlightened about shrinking so that other people won't feel insecure around you. We were born to make manifest the glory of God that is within us. It's not just in some of us, it's in everyone. And as we let our light shine, we unconsciously give other people permission to do the same. As we are liberated from our own fear, our presence liberates others."

Marian Williamson

Economic Wisdom

Live within your means. Eschew consumer debt at all costs. My in-laws Giles and Audrey Royster are a great example of economic wisdom. They believed in paying cash and putting money into savings. They raised five children on that philosophy and provided college money for all their children. When Mr. Royster bought a car he paid cash. He immediately started saving for his next car. Why pay the bank interest? They used their cash and save philosophy throughout their working lives and even into retirement.

We can live within our means and be happy as long as our eyes are not bigger than our stomachs.

The Value of Character

You can have character or be a "character". Character in a positive sense is a calling card trait. Who you are as perceived by others sets the table for many social and business interactions.

Martin Luther King in his "I have a dream" speech spoke of people being judged not by the color of their skin but the content of their character. That translates into accepting you for who you are not for what you look like.

Kindly Attitude

In a simpler time this is called being polite. In these times of "keeping it real" and in your face everything the concept can get lost. Please, thank you, or giving the benefit of the doubt along the way is a step toward a kindly attitude.

Pleasure in Work

We spend a lot of time at work. The best work is work you do for free if you could afford it. Pleasure and work may seem like an oxymoron. How can we get pleasure from working? It is all perspective. Some people actually enjoy what they do. Others not so much. For those that fall in the not so much category, there is a different approach. Think in terms of the benefits of work: food, shelter, cars, vacations etc. Pleasure may not come from work but pleasure can be gained because of work.

The Worth of Organization

The worth of organization has two perspectives. One - an organization is united in purpose or work. The shared view of the organization can enrich its members or promote an agenda that benefits its members and others.

Two – to arrange or systematize to one's benefit. In other words, get yourself together so you can find your stuff.

The Dignity of Simplicity

"All great things are simple, and many can be expressed in single words, freedom, justice, honor, duty, mercy, hope". Sir Winston Churchill

The last "inch" is as easy as KISS (Keep It Simple Simon). Life does not have to be complicated.

25

Professionalism and You

One of the great compliments in business is to be known as a professional. The following are some of the characteristics one will find in a professional.

A professional is polished.

Appearance is an essential item in being a professional. You should know what is appropriate for the type of job you seek. Bankers dress differently from graphic designers. Research your field of interest to know how to dress. I suggest you err on the side of dressing up when preparing for a job interview. If the culture is casual, you can always dress down. My father, a military man, always told me, "No matter how pressed your clothes are, it doesn't matter if your shoes are not shined." He had a mental checklist that he employed every day. The checklist can be adapted for men or women. It is nothing fancy but when followed will present a polished professional look

Hair...............neat and trimmed
Face...............shaved, teeth brushed, breath fresh
Hands............nails clean and trimmed
Clothes...........ironed, pants creased
Shoes...............shined

Your appearance is your calling card. That first impression is important. There is an old saying, "Clothes don't make the man." I agree, but a neat polished appearance doesn't hurt.

A professional is ready.

You are prepared. The moment you walk into your office or a meeting, it is go time. You have had your morning coffee, read the paper and are focused from the moment you sit down. You walk into a meeting confident, because you have done the necessary work before hand to be successful.

A professional is on time.

On time can mean different things in different countries. In the United States, it usually means you're late. Always build in a "what if" factor. What if traffic backs up? What if it snows? What if....? When you're early, use the time productively.

A professional is fair.

Your heart is your guide. Do the right thing.

A professional is energetic.

You have to have energy to get things done. Hard work without energy equals no work. An energetic professional's attitude is positive, confident, and persistent.

A professional is savvy.

A professional reads for content and pleasure. You are knowledgeable about your industry. You understand who you are and how what you do fits into the world around you.

A **professional is sincere.**

You are committed to your work. When you present an idea, you are authentic. There are no fingers crossed, or winks to get people to read between the lines. You mean what you say.

A **professional is introspective.**

You look inward to see how your actions affect the world around you. You also look inward, as a regular self-check on how you feel about yourself.

A **professional is observant.**

You are aware of your surroundings. You are sensitive to body language and territorial defenses. You see, and you learn.

A **professional networks.**

You understand how business, social and personal relationships can benefit you and others. You understand all encounters have networking possibilities. You are always prepared with a business or social card.

A **professional is assertive.**

You stand up for your point of view. Your research and reasoned thought supports your opinion. You can confidently state your case and explain your actions.

A **professional listens.**

Your strongest characteristic is listening. You can engage in a dialogue, but you are willing to withhold any comments until you thoroughly understand what you are hearing. You ask questions for clarification, but mostly you listen. This trait when combined with the other elements of professionalism, will set you apart from other business people.

A professional runs the gamut from being polished to being a good listener. All of these traits are a powerful combination. Therefore, a professional is a powerful individual. You are a powerful individual.

26

Unleashing the Power of Your Name

"What's in a name? That which we call a rose by
any other name would smell as sweet."
Romeo and Juliet (Act II, SCII)
William Shakespeare

What's in a name? We ordinarily do not think of names for more than getting someone's attention or as a means of differentiating one person from another. What's in a name? The history of surnames is quite interesting. There are six different classifications of surnames. I am sure their origin will be as fascinating to you as they are for me. Can you determine how or where your surname may originate?

Classifications of surnames.

Patronyms – derived from paternal descent. Richard's son equals Richardson.

Locative – attached to a particular place. Abraham from Lincoln equals Abraham Lincoln.

Toponym – landscape features. Jack from the rivers equals Jack Rivers.

Epithets – personal characteristics of the person. He is a long fellow equals Longfellow. Brown hair equals Brown.

Nicknames – Exaggerated substitutes or shorter versions of names. Slim or Tubby. Robert equals Rob, Bob or Bobby.

Occupational – One who cures animal skins = Tanner. A blacksmith equals Smith.

There are many colorful names that we accept without thinking. Can you match these names below?

• The Brown Bomber	• Joe DiMaggio
• The Rock	• Madonna
• Joltin' Joe	• Dwayne Johnson
• Twiggy	• Joe Louis
• The Material Girl	• Leslie Hornsby

What's in a name? My first name, Russell, is an old French nickname Rousel "little red one" (a diminutive of Rous, red, from Latin russus). Maybe the first Russell was a redhead.

What's in a name? My sister has a remarkable first and middle name – Dresden Aurelia. I can honestly say she and her name are one of a kind.

Let's have some fun. First, let me reveal I am an acronymophile. I like forming words from initials or groups of letters into a set phrase or series of words. An acronym is a word like scuba – **s**elf-**c**ontained **u**nderwater **b**reathing **a**pparatus.

You can unleash the power in your name as a powerful self-affirming acronym. Here is the two-step process:

1. Choose a positive descriptive word for each letter of your name.
2. Describe yourself as: I am (<u>using the words you have chosen to describe you</u>).

Let's try my name: Russell.

I am
Respectful **U**nderstanding **S**killed **S**uave **E**nergetic **L**oving
Liberated

Pretty cool huh? I also have developed my name into a powerful personal statement.

Reach **U**pward. **S**tand **S**trong. **E**mbrace **L**ife's **L**argesse.

Do not be afraid to ham it up. It is your name, have fun with it. You are who you say you are. I have compiled a list that you can use to unleash the power of your name. The list is not comprehensive, but it will give you a start.

Active	Adventurous	Assertive	Awesome
Bold	Brave	Blessed	Beautiful
Caring	Concerned	Cool	Committed
Daring	Driven	Dutiful	Dependable
Exciting	Enthusiastic	Energetic	Encouraging
Fun	Fearless	Faithful	Flirtatious
Genuine	Generous	Gallant	Groovy
Happy	Harmonious	Helpful	Heroic
Inquisitive	Inspired	Informed	Introspective
Juicy	Joyful	Jazzy	Jaunty
Keen	Know How	Kind	Kissable
Lovable	Liked	Lucky	Lighthearted
Magnificent	Magical	Mature	Marvelous

Nice	Natural	Nifty	Nurturing
Optimistic	Original	Observant	Outstanding
Pretty	Polite	Prepare	Personable
Quiet	Quick	Quaint	Queenly
Reserved	Resilient	Respected	Responsible
Smart	Sensible	Serious	Sexy
Tough	Tender	Ticklish	Talkative
Unstoppable	Upbeat	Unafraid	Understanding
Vibrant	Vivacious	Vigilant	Visionary
Wonderful	Warm	Watchful	Witty
Exhilarating	Experienced	Expressive	Extraordinary
Youthful	Yours	Yummy	Young
Zen	Zany	Zippy	Zesty

There is power in your name, unleash it with a powerful self-affirming acronym or a powerful personal statement.

27

Relationship Building

A relationship at its simplest is a connection between two people. The complexity of a relationship is defined by many variables, whether in a business setting, social interactions or our personal lives.

Everyone wants to be connected to someone. There are however recluses and people who want to be left alone. They are exceptions. Even then, they have some interaction with others. Unless you live in a cave and grow your own food, you will have a relationship with someone or something.

We connect with people that we can talk to. We connect with people we trust. We connect with people we like. We connect with people who like us. We connect with people who listen to us. We connect with people that support us. We connect with people who help us get what we want. We connect with people who need our help.

We build our relationships through communications and trust.

Communication is our ability to transmit ideas or messages to another person. Elements of communication include dialogue and listening. How does this work? Have a conversation – plain old simple talking. The key is having a two-way conversation with the give and take. That means one person has to listen, while the other person is talking. The person talking has the responsibility of checking to see if the message is clear. Next, be willing to listen to the other person's response and point of view. The conversation goes back and forth until the issue is accepted or mutually rejected. Or, the famous agree to disagree.

Some conversations are getting to know you conversations. We share and receive information to see if we have anything in common with the person we've just met. If so, those common interests create a connection, and we can build our relationship from there.

When we talk with others, our body language will help the connection or hinder it. Paying attention by looking at the speaker helps us connect. Looking around, shifting about, and intermittent eye contact does not.

Another element of communication is the ability to verbalize expectations. Any relationship, whether business, social or personal benefits from spoken expectations. Spoken expectations means a person does not have to read your mind. You give the other person a chance to accept, reject or suggest a compromise to your expectations. That brings us back to a conversation – plain old simple talking.

Trust in a business setting manifests itself as confidence in the person. Trust in social or personal settings may be seen as faith or belief in someone we can depend on.

Who do you trust? Who do you confide in? You trust and confide in the person with whom you have built a relationship. So how do we become confident, have faith, believe in or depend on someone? We set boundaries. We expect full disclosure.

Setting boundaries in a relationship creates freedom. It may sound limiting, but it is not. Boundaries establish where a relationship is solid. Living outside the boundaries will damage our confidence, our faith, our beliefs and our dependence.

Have you ever told someone you trust a secret? Only to discover your secret was shared with someone else? Your trust was compromised because that person went outside your relationship boundaries.

Full disclosure is telling all of the truth. It is that simple. It is that simple because in building relationships, we are constantly talking to each other. We share our expectations. We share our confidence, faith, and beliefs. We depend on each other. We respect the boundaries of the relationship. Therefore, we are not going to do anything we cannot tell.

There is a question lingering out there. What if we damage our relationship? What do we do? There is no simple answer. Some relationships will not recover. However, the fundamentals to rebuilding relationships are the same ones used to build relationships.

When we communicate and show trust in our relationships, we are doing our part. Always do your part.

28

Put it in Writing

Put it in writing is a catchall phrase. I will use it for two different applications. One is put it in writing for business reasons, and the other is put it in writing for personal reasons.

There was a time that a look in the eye, a promise given and a handshake would seal a deal. Our culture today has strayed from that simple way of doing business. Contracts are the legal way to document agreements. My take on this is personal, any legal advice you need should come from a lawyer.

I have signed many contracts over the years – mostly real estate contracts. The one thing I know is to read the fine print, and that is not easy. There is enough archaic language in some real estate contracts to make a grown man cry. And for the most part, I have breezed through with the notion – "Do not miss a payment and I will be fine." That is not the best way, but it has worked for me. The fun part of real estate contracts for me is making an offer or counter offer. One thing you'll notice is that these offers or counter offers are not oral. We put them in writing and sign them to acknowledge our seriousness.

Think of how retailers use documentation to sell goods. They put warranties in writing stating what they will or will not do over the working life of a product. Many consumers have purchased products because of the promise in writing the manufacturer has made.

Business loves documentation. Strategic thinking manifests itself in business plans. Business plans are written documentation of someone's idea to make a company flourish. Any entrepreneur will tell you, they cannot borrow money without a business plan. They can walk into a bank with an idea, but will not receive any money until they put it in writing.

You cannot return an item unless you have written or printed documentation – a receipt.

Who am I? Let me give you my printed documentation – my resume or my business card.

How did my business do last year? Let me give you my printed documentation – the annual report.

How did I perform on my job this year? Let me give you written documentation – my performance appraisal.

What's wrong with my car? Please give me written documentation – an estimate or a condition report.

Everywhere we go, someone is putting a promise or request in writing. For the most part, it is a good thing, but read the fine print.

I first thought writing a personal narrative only happened with the girls. It seemed they were the only ones putting anything in writing. When I was growing up, they were keeping personal diaries. Nowhere did I see any boys writing down their thoughts daily. Later, I heard about keeping a journal. At the time, I thought that was the male equivalent of a diary. Of course, anyone can have a diary or a journal. The key is taking the time to record – document – put in writing what you think is important. There are several approaches for writing in diaries or journals.

One approach is a stream of consciousness. Whatever comes to your mind, you write. Stream of consciousness is a free flowing form of expression. There is no editing, or worry about content. You just write until you have nothing else to say.

Another approach is to answer a series of questions. Your questions may be different. Customize your questions to fit your needs.

Morning:
What do I want to accomplish today?
What is most important?
Who can I help today?
Who do I ask for help today?

Evening:
What did I accomplish today?
Did I meet my goals?
How do I feel about myself?

The next approach is sequential. You log or record your actions with or without commentary.

- The day's activities by time.
- Daily calorie intake.
- Exercises in workout routine daily.
- Books read.
- Medication taken.

Keeping a diary or journal can be fun. It is up to you, what you write about.

There are still people out there who will take your word and seal it with a handshake. But for all others, put it in writing.

29

Old School

Old school means different things to different people. Old school for me was the preteen years 11 and 12 to late 20s. It was a time of awakening and growth. I can remember my parents recalling their old school days. They listened to Ella Fitzgerald, The Platters, Ray Charles and watched movies with Leno Horne, Cab Calloway and the Nicholas Brothers.

Old school memories are shared memories. For baby boomers, who can forget the styles, the music, the dances, and the history of our time?

What about those old school values from back in the day? Old school values never change. I was taught to say, "No sir, no ma'am, yes sir, yes ma'am, please and thank you." Old school values reflect respect for your elders, family and friends. It is not difficult to simply be polite.

Here is how times are really different. Back in the day, discipline was immediate. If a child acted up, it was nothing to be on the business end of a switch or belt. The saying – "spare the rod spoil the child", was in full force. The enforcement of discipline extended to my parents friends. If they saw me get into mischief or acting up, they had permission to discipline me and send me home. Now, that's the true meaning of: "It takes a village to raise a child". Let me say this before you call Child Services. It was not abuse. It was a way to shape behaviour. The consequences were soon and certain and deserved.

Fortunately some of the values from back in the day are still meaningful. Today we still value God, family and country. Some things never go out of style.

What about education back in the day? We learned the fundamentals. We had no choice. There was no guarantee of college. High school students had to graduate with the skills to make a living.

The three R's: reading, 'riting and 'rithmetic were fundamental staples of a good education. We read to learn how to read. Reading out loud also helped diction. We learned to read by reading for pleasure and not just for content.

The library was a source of magic. Rows and rows of books transported us around the world. I enjoy the immediacy of the Internet for information but there's nothing like holding and reading a book.

Education back in the day taught penmanship and problem solving. I can remember in a math class being told getting the right answer is not enough. We had to show the work so that we could prove our answer was not a lucky guess.

What happened to shop classes or home economics? I know we have computer technology today and that is progress. We learned in high school how to work with our hands, how to build shelves or bend metal. It really comes in handy today for home projects.

What about music back in the day? There is no music like the music of your teenage years and your young adult years. I am going to go out on a limb and say Motown, the Philly sound, the British Invasion, Rock and Roll and Country Western were the best in the sixties and seventies. There I said it and I am sticking to it.

Motown Records - founded by Berry Gordy.

The Temptations, The Marvelettes, Gladys Knight and the Pips, Martha Reeves and the Vandellas, Mary Wells, Diana Ross and the Supremes, The Four Tops, Stevie Wonder, Commodores,

Jr. Walker and the All Stars, The Jackson Five, Smokey Robinson and the Miracles and Marvin Gaye.

Philadelphia International Records – founded by Ken Gamble and Leon Huff.

The Delfonics, The Stylistics, The O'Jays, The Spinners, Teddy Pendergrass, TSOP (The Sound of Philadelphia), Billy Paul and Lou Rawls.

Rock and Roll

Beach Boys, McCoys, Four Seasons, Carole King, Paul Revere and the Raiders, Mamas and the Papas, Turtles, Jefferson Airplane, Doors, The Who, Led Zeppelin, Kinks, Three Dog Night, Doobie Brothers, Chicago, Badfinger, Steve Miller Band, Lynyrd, Skynyrd, Bee Gees, Queen, Foreigner, Kansas, Marshall Tucker, Eagles, Fleetwood Mac, The Knack, KC and the Sunshine Band and Credence Clearwater Revival.

The British Invasion

The Beatles, The Rolling Stones, The Dave Clark Five, The Sex Pistols, The Clash, Squeeze, Elvis Costello and the Attractions.

Country Western

Kenny Rogers, Barbara Mandrel, Waylon Jennings, Willie Nelson, Ronnie Milsap, Johnny Rodriguez, Tanya Tucker, Charley Pride, Loretta Lynn, Conway Twitty, Tammy Wynette, Jeannie C. Riley, Dolly Parton, Hank Williams Jr., Dottie West, Loretta Lynn, Lynn Anderson and Olivia Newton-John.

All World Old School back in the day

Aretha Franklin, James Brown, Marvin Gaye, Stevie Wonder, Bruce Springsteen, Isaac Hayes, Barry White, Sly and the Family

Stone, Willie Nelson, Gloria Gaynor, Ray Charles, Elvis Presley, Jerry Lee Lewis, Smokey Robinson, Everly Brothers, Johnny Cash, Elton John, Sam Cooke, Arthur Prysock, Michael Jackson and Prince.

I know this is not everyone, I know I named some people twice. That's alright. You get my drift.

What about games back in the day? Monopoly, Scrabble, Operation, Concentration, The Game of Life, Stratego, Hopscotch, Horseshoes, Jarts, Hula Hoops, Parcheesie, Candyland, Connect Four, Yahtzee, Password and Battleship.

What about clothing style back in the day? Bell bottoms, short miniskirts, hot pants, platform shoes, dashikis, kaftans, tank tops, maxi skirts, leisure suits, white suits, gold chains, bright colors, satin fabrics, wide brim hats, tie dye t-shirts, head bands, NBA shorts, wide lapels, open collar shirts, halter tops, Nehru jackets, and jeans.

What about history back in the day? The 60's and 70's were an amazing time in our history. The following highlights of history are what I remember:

My earliest historical memory - I remember John F. Kennedy being elected (November 1960). I was in the third grade and attending St Joseph's, a parochial school in Meridian, Mississippi. The nuns were excited about the first Catholic elected President.

11/22/63 – John F Kennedy assassinated in Dallas. We were stunned as a nation.

4/30/67 – Cassius Clay (later known as Muhammad Ali) was stripped of his championship boxing title because he refused to be inducted into military service.

6/06/67 – Bobby Kennedy (brother of the late John F. Kennedy and presidential candidate) was killed.

12/03/67 – five surgeons headed by Dr Christian N. Barnard performed the first heart transplant.

4/05/68 – Martin Luther King killed at the Lorraine Motel in Memphis, Tennessee. My introduction to civil rights nationally.

9/09/68 – Arthur Ashe became the first African American to win the US Open Tennis Championship.

10/27/68 – The Summer Olympics. Tommy Smith and John Carlos placed first and third in the 200 meters track event. They were suspended for accepting medals with the black power salute.

1/12/69 – Broadway Joe Namath and the New York Jets beat the heavily favored Baltimore Colts for the Super Bowl Championship.

7/20/69 Neil Armstrong was the first man to walk on the moon. He was later joined by Edwin Aldrin.

8/17/69 – Thousands flocked to the musical event of the century – The Woodstock Festival.

5/7/70 – The Kent State shootings. National guardsmen fired into a crowd of Kent State University student protestors, killing four people and wounding eight others.

1/27/73 – Truce agreement to end the Vietnam War. The cease-fire went into effect at seven o'clock. The war ranged from 1965 – 1973.

8/08/74 – President Nixon resigns as President of the United States. He is succeeded and eventually pardoned of any crimes by Vice President Gerald Ford.

7/04/74 – The United States celebrated its bi-centennial.

3/28/77 – The worst aviation disaster in history. 547 passengers and crew died when two 747 jumbo jets collided.

7/25/78 – The first test tube baby is born in London.

3/31/79 – Egypt and Israel agree to a historic peace treaty. It was signed by Egypt's President Anwar el-Sadat, Israel Prime Minister Menachem Begin and witnessed by United States President Jimmy Carter.

Old School memories can bring tears of joy and sadness. Most of all, Old School back in the day memories are special.

Old School was a groove
From a funky move
To what we would say
Way back in the day

From music to school
It was always cool
Nice in every way
Way back in the day.

Your time is coming
When tunes you're humming
Make you smile and say
This is how we rolled
Way back in my day

30

Speak without Fear

The fear of speaking in public is called glossophobia. It is believed to be the single most common phobia – affecting as much of 75 percent of the population. So what do you do if you're not in the 25 percent who love speaking in front of others but want to give it a try?

My method is called PRIME WAVES. I imagine the calming effect of the ocean. I imagine the ebb and flow of the tide. PRIME WAVES represents the steps you can take to speak without fear.

Preparation

Lack of preparation to speak causes the most anxiety. Gather your research and edit that information into your presentation or speech. You will have accomplished the most important part in speaking without fear.

Rehearsal

Can you imagine a team playing without practice? Practice. Practice. Practice. Use all of the time you have wisely. Do not wait until the last minute. Your rehearsal time is the time to make and correct mistakes. The written word does not always flow as easily as the spoken word. Rehearsal is where you find out what works.

Identify anxiety as excitement.

Instead of letting anxiety sap your stress use it as energy. Use your anxiety as an adrenaline rush. Think of the thrill of riding a roller coaster. Feel the tingles that let you know you are alive. That's excitement. Use it to get yourself pumped up for your audience.

Manage your breathing.

You have your adrenaline pumping – BREATH!! It is hard to believe but sometimes we hold our breath when we are excited. Breathe in through your nose and slowly out from your mouth. As you breathe in, your stomach should expand. That means you are collecting air in your diaphragm and not your chest. In slowly, out slowly. You are at peace.

Expect Success

You are your own self-fulfilling prophecy. You will do well because you expect to do well. What else could happen? You have prepared and rehearsed. Piece of cake!!

Warm up your voice and body

The warm up loosens you up. If you are able to be alone before your speech, stretch a bit. Recite the alphabet; make faces to warm up your face. If you are seated with your audience or on stage then warm up before you are seated. You are like an athlete that needs to warm up before you are ready to go.

Affirm your Self

Tell yourself – I am a good speaker
I have information that will help my audience
I prepare well for speeches
I passionately rehearse my speeches
I am excited to give this speech

Visualize your audience

Your research and rehearsal preparation is physical. Visualization is a powerful tool. It is a mental rehearsal of your speech, the venue and your audience. Visualization gives you the feeling of having been there before. Your performance will be natural and comfortable because of your mental preparation.

Emphasize eye contact

Eye contact is your visual connection to your audience. If you are in a large venue you may not see the audience. Many speeches are given in a smaller more personal setting. Look at a member of your audience say a few words then move on. Make eye contact with someone else, say a few words and move on. Repeat this technique throughout your speech.

Speak from your heart

Your heart represents love and authenticity. It does not matter if it is a business speech or an entertaining speech. You have to keep it real. Share your stories and connect with your audience. The speech is not about you, the speech is for your audience. You don't talk to...you talk with. You don't tell...you share. You don't take from your audience...you give.

Though I speak with the tongues of men and of angels, and have not charity, I am become as sounding brass, or a tinkling cymbal.

I Corinthians 13:1

Use PRIME WAVES as your guide and turn your fear of speaking into the joy of speaking.

31

Expand your Memory

One of the biggest complaints I hear is from people who say, "I've a terrible memory." "I'm always forgetting things." "I'd forget my own nose if it wasn't attached to my face."

"Really", I respond, "and do you ever forget to go to work in the morning?" They look at me as if I am crazy. "Of course not," they reply. "Well then your memory isn't as bad as you're making out. In spite of what you might think, you do not have a bad memory. You simply have an untrained one."

"Hmmm," I hear you thinking, "Untrained memory. I don't like the sound of the word untrained. It brings the words 'trained' and 'training' to mind. Sounds like hard work to me."

Congratulations if you can identify with that last sentence. You are already half way to having a measurably improved memory. Let me explain.

Let's say that right now you aren't very fit and you decide you want to run a marathon. So what are you going to do? To successfully achieve that goal you will need to change your diet and start exercising and training. There are months of training too, and most of it hard work. A worthy physical goal will increase your self-confidence and self-esteem.

So what does this training bring to mind? Yes, a change of diet. You can eat more protein, eliminate junk foods from your eating plan or perhaps get up an hour earlier for a five mile run. After a

while, you can extend it to ten miles. Visualize yourself in your shorts, shirt and running shoes, sprinting all over the neighborhood at ungodly hours. So much sweat pouring out of you, it would fill a bucket. Feel the aches and pains in your muscles and cramps in your legs and feet.

Right now, you might be shaking in your boots. "If I have to go through a similar routine to improve my memory, I'm out of here." Is that what you're thinking? Relax. In comparison to running a marathon, improving your memory is both easy and simple. And you're already familiar with the first step!

Here is the big secret to all memory training. You use something you already know to remind you of something you don't know. That's it. All trained memory is using one thing to remind you of another. Now there are both simple and advanced methods for doing this but each and every one of them uses the principle of using "A" to remind you of "B" and "B" to remind you of "C".

You may not realize it but we've already done that. In our example above the word "UNTRAINED" brings to mind the words "TRAINED" and "TRAINING". Those words bring to mind physical exercise and the image of you running through the neighborhood filling a bucket full of sweat.

You see how one word leads to another and forms a mental image?

Let's look at a couple more examples. And I'm serious when I say a simple understanding of this point will make the rest of this chapter incredibly easy for you.

In fact memory systems are so simple, you may not even bother to use them. "What?" I hear you ask. Well the first and most obvious question is, "If these systems are so simple, why aren't they taught in schools?" It is truly amazing that a child will go to school for twelve to fourteen years and every day the teachers are heaping on more and more information without ever giving a system for remembering it.

Imagine a lawyer's office with all his documents heaped all over the floor. He's up to his waist in papers. If you were to come in now and develop a system, here's what you would probably do. Sort the documents. Put similar papers (property transactions for example) in one section. Then sort the first section, assembling the papers into bundles, one bundle for each client. Then put the papers for that bundle in the correct order, place them in a folder and file it in a cabinet.

One thing you can be sure of. That lawyer's office contains all his papers. The problem is organizing them so the required information is easily accessible. It's almost the same with our school pupil. All the information is there. She simply needs a method for sorting what's important, locking it in and remembering it accurately.

So why aren't such methods taught in schools? I don't know. It would make teachers' lives so much easier and pupils would learn and understand so much more. Perhaps, it's to do with the Victorian attitude that nothing is worthwhile unless you've suffered to achieve it.

Either way these simple but powerful methods are yours to use. They can be traced back at least as far as the ancient Greeks and Romans and are the same methods used by world memory champions to recall shuffled decks of playing cards and long lists of random numbers and items.

While winning the world memory championships will certainly bring a level of fame and honors, I don't feel it has much practical use for you. Certainly a memory exercise remembering random lists is useful. But I would argue that if you're going to remember a list you may as well remember a useful one. Surely remembering the list of towns in your geographical area or facts about an upcoming holiday destination will be more useful than twenty random objects.

I will give you at the end of this book a memory system that is very practical for remembering any ten items. As a bonus you can use it as a party piece to show off in front of your friends. You will be able to recite the list of ten random objects both forwards and backwards as well as in and out of order. Besides, being extremely useful in real life is a great way to practice. And your friends will think you are a mental genius!

You're stuck in the jungle and you have a machete. You can use it to hack your way through the undergrowth, taking weeks to get through, or you can find a fallen log, sit on it and float down the river, allowing the natural flow of the water to take you to your destination. With memory systems, you will simply use the way your mind already works – it'll be just like floating down the river.

Or think of it like this: I give you a can of paint and ask you to open it by prying the lid off. You can really mess up your fingers and even if you get the lid open, the chances are you'll spill some of the paint in doing so. But if I give you a spoon and you use the base of the handle as a lever to pry off the lid, it is so much easier. No fuss and no mess.

Learning by rote is like opening a can of paint with your fingers. Using a lever is like using trained memory systems.

But I digress. Let's get back to the two examples I was giving you.

You're at a function. It's busy, lots of people, lots of chat. Suddenly you become aware of an unusual smell - a pleasant scent. You recognise it from somewhere. But where? A warm fuzzy feeling runs through your body and vivid pictures fill your mind. It's your grandmother. That's her scent. The perfume she always wore. She's been dead for years now and suddenly, out of the blue - here's that same scent. Pictures of your grandmother fill your mind. You remember her kindness and love, the things you did together and playing with her dog. You remember that she never forgot your birthday and the little presents she had for you whenever she saw you. You remember the fun times you had when you stayed with her and grandfather for your holidays. You remember how your grandfather took you fishing and the thrill of the first fish you ever caught. The emotion grips you and your eyes well up with tears.

That chain of events and every one of those memories were brought to mind by the perfume someone was wearing at the function. It brought to mind in great detail a number of other events.

Here is another example. You're at a dinner party and someone asks if you've ever done scuba diving? Yes, you reply. I went scuba diving in Malta. "Where's Malta?" If you studied geography in school, you will know that Italy is in the shape of a boot. Just off the toe of the boot, in the middle of the Mediterranean Sea, is the large triangular shaped island of Sicily. Just below Sicily is the small island of Malta. You continue telling of the two weeks you spent there scuba diving, finding a baby octopus, its tentacles clinging to your hand, finding a sunken ship, and diving at night in a thunderstorm. And of course the places you visited in Malta, the craft shops, the catacombs where St Paul stayed when he was shipwrecked there, the splendour of each village's church, and the medieval fortified city of Valetta.

From these two examples you can see how one thing leads to another and opens up a whole scenario. The scent reminds you of your grandmother, her kindness, her home, your grandfather, and catching your first fish. Scuba diving reminds you of where you went diving and a whole scenario of events and places.

This is the way your mind naturally works. One thought, one idea leads to another, and another and another. And all we do with memory systems is to make use of the way the mind naturally works. Instead of forcing ourselves to learn long lists of information by rote, we're going to arrange the information and link it to something we already know, making recall both instant and accurate.

NATURAL ASSOCIATIONS

Your mind naturally makes associations with what interests it. Watch an eight year old boy who is passionate about baseball or football. He will listen to the scores on television and instantly be able to repeat them. He will know all the teams in the league and the names and positions of their key players. He will know the names and details of all the players in his favorite team.

Give him a talk on the geography of somewhere alien to him - say - Outer Mongolia - and he won't be able to repeat a word of it. However if you were to tell him of how they play a similar game to baseball in Outer Mongolia, you'd have his attention.

Compare his type of baseball with the Mongolian kind. Explain how some players in Mongolia have amazing stamina because their geographical region is so mountainous you can only play on a slope, so when they play on the flat, they have an advantage over regular players. Other players can run faster for longer because they come from an area where they catch live rabbits by hand and they've been doing this since the age of six.

Suddenly your young friend is developing an interest and knowledge of the geography of Outer Mongolia. You have framed the information into such a way that it's linked to something he already knows. Because of that, it is information he will retain.

It may sound like I'm belaboring this. It is vital you grasp the concept that all that memory systems require is adding something you know to something you don't know in a way that allows for accurate recall.

We know that memory systems have been around for thousands of years and were widely used by the ancient Greeks and Romans.

You're already familiar with some memory systems, though you may not realize it. We've already mentioned what every school child knows – Italy is in the shape of a boot. You might be familiar with the acronym **HOMES**. An acronym is where you take the first letter of each of your list of words and form them into a different word. In this case each letter represents the first letter of each of the Great Lakes of North America,

Huron **O**ntario **M**ichigan **E**rie **S**uperior

Or perhaps the age-old rhyme for remembering the days in each month:

Thirty days hath September
April, June and November.
All the rest have thirty-one
Excepting February alone,
Which has twenty-eight days clear,

But twenty-nine each Leap Year.

These three examples are easy and simple memory hooks. If you learned them as a child, you still remember them. For some reason it never seems to have dawned on educators to use the same process for all the other information you have to learn, not just for school and college but any trade, business or sport you might get into.

Every vocation or hobby has its own vocabulary, specific to that field of interest. So remembering new information is an ongoing and lifelong experience, not simply a requirement for school subjects. And what's more it's FUN!

Perhaps you might want to give a speech without notes, recall technical details for a sales presentation, or simply show off your ability to recall lists of information. Keep reading and you'll discover how.

The three examples given above all use a different technique. The first is visual. You can picture a boot in your mind and therefore ITALY. The second brings to mind the word HOMES which then gives us the names of the lakes. The third uses the natural rhythm of the words to make the days in the month memorable.

We'll now look at extending these techniques and adding to them, so that by the end of the book, your friends will view you as a memory expert, able to recall huge chunks of information and numbers, as well as remembering the names of people you meet.

YOUR FIRST STEP TO REMEMBERING ANYTHING

This is so simple and it gets overlooked by 90% of the people who try memory systems. And it may surprise you. The first step is to pay attention to the information you want to remember. Observe it. That's all. Take a moment to really look it. Not what you think it is or what it might be.

Have a look at the following:

**PARIS
IN THE
THE SPRING**

If you said "Paris in the spring" you are mistaken. Have another look. Did you catch that the word "the" appears twice? That's why it's vital to observe the information properly. Otherwise our brains may see what they want or expect to see. You really must pay attention, break it down, analyze it. Are there any patterns emerging? Does it sound like something you already know? How does it look visually?

If you get false information embedded in your mind it can be next to impossible to replace it with the correct data. Take the story of the Tom the schoolboy who constantly got the year wrong of when Columbus discovered America. "1493," he'd say. Eventually the school teacher gave him a rhyme. "In 1492, Columbus crossed the ocean blue."

The next day the teacher asked Tom, "What year did Columbus discover America?" "1493." he answered. "What about the rhyme I gave you, Tom?" the teacher asked. "In 1493, Columbus crossed the deep blue sea."

So be careful you're inputting accurate facts!

A good few years ago a friend had a six digit telephone number 784337. He told all his friends that it was easy to remember. "Just recall the 'Stupid Cannibal'," he'd say. "Seven Ate Four, Three and Three ate Seven."

Just by taking a moment to pay attention to the number gave him the memory hook. You'd be surprised just how often taking a moment to accurately observe the information will prompt a memory hook. There may be a natural recurring pattern, an odd shape that might remind you of something. Saying it aloud may reveal a natural rhythm in the words.

Stalactites and Stalagmites

In caves you will see rock formations that hang down from the ceiling and reach up from the ground. These are called Stalactites and Stalagmites but how can you remember which is which?

Let's take it in steps. First, observe the words. Is there anything we can associate with to remind us of which is which? Yes there is!

stalaGmite - stalaCtite = Ground and Ceiling

StalaCtites drop from the Ceiling and StalaGmites rise up from the Ground.

OK. You've looked at the information and there doesn't appear to be any logical memory hook. What then?

Simple, we make one up.

I know it sounds silly but some school teachers do teach their pupils to use simple memory systems. They teach ones they already know, but it never seems to dawn on them that it's just as easy to come up with your own. You don't have to wait for someone else to think them up.

Now we'll look at the three main methods for remembering words and information.

The first is acronyms. This is perfect for lists of words that do not have to be remembered in order. HOMES is a perfect example. Another is for the twelve European countries that use the EURO as their currency. A very handy acronym for your next European holiday! It's BAFFLING PIGS

Belgium
Austria
France
Finland
Luxembourg
Ireland
Netherlands
Germany

Portugal
Italy
Greece
Spain

ROY G. BIV for the colours of the spectrum in order:
Red Orange Yellow Green Blue Indigo Violet

The Seven Processes of Life: **MRS. GERN** (or **MRS. NERG**)

Movement Reproduction Sensitivity Growth Excretion Respiration Nutrition

You can also use an acrostic. While an acronym uses one or two words to remember a list of words, an acrostic is where a full sentence provides the hook to remember a list of words, usually in sequence.

To remember: the classification system for living things from Biology take -

King **P**hilip **C**an **O**nly **F**ind **G**reen **S**lippers. The first letter of each word will remind you of the first letter of: Kingdom Phylum Class Order Family Genus Species.

Continue for the classification for humans:

Anthropology Can Make People Hate Helping the Sick

Anamalia **C**ordata **M**amalia **P**rimate **H**ominidae **H**omo **S**apiens

The British Royal House Families can be remembered like this:

No Plan Like Yours To Study History Wisely

This translates into:

Normandy, **P**lantagenet, **L**ancaster, **Y**ork, **T**udor, **S**tuart, **H**anover, **W**indsor

You may never have the inclination to recall the British Royal House Families. That's not the point. The point is to show you how these principles can be used by you for any such list you might want to remember.

You Can Use It For Spelling:

Geography: **G**eorge **E**dward's **O**ld **G**randma **R**ode **A** **P**ony **H**ome **Y**esterday

Arithmetic: **A** **R**at **I**n **T**he **H**ouse **M**ay **E**at **T**he **I**ce **C**ream

Difficulty: Mr **D**, Mr **I**, Mr **FFI**, Mr **C**, Mr **U**, Mr **LTY** (say it aloud)

Saskatchewan: **Ask At Chew An** with an **S** in front of it.

Here's one to remember the countries of Central America in geographical order:

BeeGee's Elastic Hen!

Now see 'er pee? It sounds crazy and unusual but that's what makes it easy to remember.

The bland and the ordinary are difficult to recall. Making the sentence funny and unusual actually makes it easy to remember.

Bee (Belize)
Gee (Guatemala)
Elastic (El Salvador)
Hen (Honduras)
Now (Nicaragua)
See 'er (C R - Costa Rica)
Pee (Panama)

The Confederate States of America: Mississippi Virginia, North Carolina, South Carolina, Louisiana, Georgia, Alabama, Arkansas, Tennessee, Florida, and Texas.

Misses Virginia and Carol (North and South) Loved George, Always Arguing Tenth Floor Taxes.

To remember the planets in order from the sun

"My Very Excellent Mother Just Sent Us Nine Pizzas"

Mercury **V**enus **E**arth **M**ars **J**upiter **S**aturn **U**ranus **N**eptune **P**luto

Or perhaps you want to remember the planets from the smallest to the largest:

Pluto Must Meet Venus Every Night Until Saturn Jumps

Pluto Mercury Mars Venus Earth Neptune Uranus Saturn Jupiter

Bible Studies

There is no end to the uses for memory systems. Here are two methods for recalling the names of the twelve apostles. (In the second example don't be confused because Simon Peter is frequently known as just Peter).

Bartholomew, Andrew, John, Phillip, Thomas, Matthew, James, James the Younger, Simon the Zealot, Simon Peter, Judas (sometimes known as Thaddeus) and Judas Iscariot

Mnemonic 1:

Bart (Bartholomew) **and** (Andrew) **John fill** (Phillip) **Tom's mat** (Matthew) **with 2 James's, 2 Simons, and 2 Judas's.**"

Mnemonic 2:

"This is the way the disciples run
Peter, Andrew, James, John Phillip and Bartholomew
Thomas next and Matthew, too.
James the less and Judas the greater
Simon the zealot and Judas the traitor."

So there you have a number of solid and trusted examples on using acronyms and acrostics. Pretty much any list of words can be recalled using this system. Now that you have grasped the power of this principle, why not put it to work to remember your own lists?

You'll notice that the anagram/acrostic system seems best for words with which you're already familiar. Suppose you need to recall really weird sounding words or foreign language vocabulary?

Foreign Language Vocabulary

With abstract words and foreign language vocabulary, it is first necessary to pause and examine the word. Look at it phonetically. What does it sound like? Does it bring a mental image to mind? What do the syllables sound like? Do they bring anything to mind? You may have to have a stretch of the imagination but does it sound like any familiar word?

It is then a matter of making a vivid mental picture linking the two together. After you have encountered the words a few times the mental image will disappear and the word become a permanent part of your vocabulary without having to think.

A few examples with English/French vocabulary:

Rug/carpet - tapis - image of an ornate oriental carpet with a tap as the central design woven in chrome thread

Grumpy - grognon - a grumpy man groaning with irritation

To tease - taquiner - a wife teasing her husband as she takes in the washing.

Sometimes the foreign language word will have a different meaning in English. For example the German word for plate is **Teller**. In English a teller works in a bank. So imagine the teller having his lunch counting out bank notes onto a plate.

You can also make a pun, or a rhyme, or a joke, an association that triggers this word in your mind. Phillip Mahnken, a language teacher from Australia suggests:

The Indonesian word for white is putih. He tells students to think of "a white putih cat."

The Indonesian word for seven is tujuh. One of his students once said: "So, on your seventh birthday, they sing "Happy birthday tujuh!""

Here's a way to remember the French verbs that are conjugated with être using our old friend the acronym:

Dr. (and) Mrs. Vandertramp

D	**devenir**
R	**revenir**
M	**mourir**
R	**retourner**
S	**sortir**
V	**venir**
A	**aller**

N	**naître**
D	**descendre**
E	**entrer**
R	**rentrer**
T	**tomber**
R	**rester**
A	**arriver**
M	**monter**
P	**partir**

For foreign language vocabulary here are the two steps we've used:

Observe it. Is there anything odd, unusual or memorable about it? Does it look or sound funny? What about the spelling? Are any letters repeated a lot?

Break it down into syllables. Say the word and the syllables aloud. What do they sound like? Do they remind you of anything? Do they remind you of any English words with similar meaning?

Make a vivid, colourful, silly mental picture. Example: The word chicken in French is **poule**. **Poule** sounds like the English word **pull**. Picture a big brown chicken pulling a bunch of other chickens along with a rope.

A third and very useful step for students is:

Look the word up in the dictionary. More often than not the word will have a root or a relation to another word you are already familiar with. You will also discover other words from the same family which has the added benefit of adding even more words to your vocabulary.

REMEMBERING A SPEECH

The ancient Greeks were excellent at giving speeches. Back then there was no radio or TV, so listening to a speech was a good way to pass an afternoon. The great orators could talk for hours without notes. One of their methods for remembering all the points they wanted to cover is what we know as the Link or Story method.

Suppose for some obscure reason you want to remember these nine counties from the South of England and you want to remember them in this particular order: Avon, Dorset, Somerset, Cornwall, Wiltshire, Devon, Gloucestershire, Hampshire, and Surrey.

All we do is link the words together into a story that is easy to visualise. The more vivid the mental images, the easier it is to remember the story.

Picture this with me as we go along and you will be able to recall those nine counties by the time we've reached the end. An AVON lady (see her with her overflowing bag of cosmetics) is knocking on a big solid DOOR (Dorset). The door swings open and you see a beautiful SUMMER (Somerset) country scene. It's evening and the sun is setting over a field of CORN (Cornwall). Picture the corn vividly in your mind. As you look closer you see the corn is WILTing (Wiltshire) and has formed the shape of a DEVil (Devon). Impaled on the devil's fork is a GLOSSy (Gloucestershire) HAM (Hampshire) SORbet (Surrey).

If you have followed along with me and visualized the scene in your mind, you must know the list of nine counties.

You'll probably never need to know the names of those counties, but you may need to know the names of your local counties, or towns in your locality. I just want to show you how simple the principle is to use.

When you come to make a speech, or give a presentation, make a list of your key points. Now pick one single word that will remind you of that point. List your words in the correct sequence. Develop a story to link the words together. Visualise the sequence in your mind.

The sillier the story the easier it is to remember. You are the only person who will know the story, so don't be embarrassed about how silly or exaggerated your mental images are.

Likewise if you have a sequence of events to remember, such as an episode from history, just make a list of key words and make a simple story to link them together.

Remembering Names and Faces

The most common memory complaint is that people can't remember names. Well, the main reason is very simple. You haven't registered it in the first place. Let's look at a typical social example. You're at a party and your host takes you over to a group of six people. She's going to introduce you to six people you've never met. Inside you're telling yourself, "I'll never remember all these names."

So what happens? You have set up a self-fulfilling prophecy. You have given yourself an internal command, which your mind makes a reality. Your host introduces everyone and after the introduction you look around the group and inner panic sets in. You can't put a name to any face. You recall that one of the names was Tom, but you're not sure whether it was the first guy or the second.

You remind yourself that you're no good at remembering names and you now have firm evidence to prove it. So, if you've proved to yourself that you can't remember names, why would you bother to try in the first place?

Let me ask you a question. Why is it that top politicians remember the names of almost everyone they meet? And they meet thousands of people regularly. Politicians' very existence depends on being able to remember names. They know that they have to remember, so they do. It's that simple.

There are many methods for remembering names and I'll give you a few of the easier ones. You can implement them immediately and see the results straight away.

But first I have to give you the most important factor in remembering names. Without this all the methods are useless. With it, you will amaze yourself, even if you don't use any of the methods.

The vital factor is the conscious intention to remember names. You must believe that you will remember the names. Visualise yourself after meeting a new group of people. Visualise yourself calling them by their first names and see in your mind's eye recalling their names after you've left the group.

I can't emphasize enough just how important this is. Imagine a soccer match where the player is going to take a penalty shot. The coach beckons to him and says, "Whatever you do, don't shoot for the top right." What happens? The player kicks the ball to the top right of the net, and the goal keeper saves it.

The coach unwittingly put a negative thought in the players mind and that thought became the dominant thought. "Top Right, Top Right, Top Right."

Your biggest obstacle to remembering names is your own belief that you can't. From now on, go out with the firm belief that you do remember names. It's not "I will remember names", which places remembering in the future. It's "I do remember names" or "I always remember names" which places it in the present.

When you're introduced to someone, take a moment to look at them properly, make a firm mental image of their face. Say his name is Tom. Make eye contact, shake hands and say something like, "Hello Tom, nice to meet you." During the first minute of conversation, use his name a couple of times and when leaving say, "Tom, it was great to meet you." You have mentioned his name a few times, which will cement it in your memory.

You might feel a little awkward mentioning his name a few times. Here's a way to use it without addressing him directly. You phrase a question as though someone else were asking it and they use his name. For example let's say Tom is a fireman. You might say, "Do people ever come up to you and say, Tom what's the most dangerous fire you've ever attended?"

Another method is to look at their face and see is there something that stands out that makes them easy to remember. Perhaps there is something about their hairstyle, their spectacles, or the size of their nose etc. That can give you a memory hook. Do they remind you of someone you already know?

When you get introduced to larger groups, you will feel a bit intimidated by having to remember six names at once. Don't bother to try and remember them all at one go. Scan the group and pick two or three of the more interesting looking people. Just remember their names. And do make a point of repeating everyone's name when you hear it, even if it slows down the introductions.

During the conversation, be sure and mention the names you know a few times. It's also quite likely that someone will call another person by name. If it's a name you missed, then here's your chance to lock it in.

It's also possible that a new person will be introduced to the group, so you have another chance to hear all the names.

You will be really surprised at how quickly you will grasp and remember names. Imagine how confident you will feel, and how impressed people will be when after you have been introduced to a group, a new person comes over and you say, "Let me introduce you to everyone." Keep that picture in your mind and it will happen.

As your confidence grows you will be easily able to remember all the names of the group.

You know how you're talking with someone and you can't remember his name? Well it stands to reason other people may be having the same problem remembering your name, doesn't it?

When Winston Churchill met people he always introduced himself, "I'm Winston Churchill."

Another method is to refer to yourself through a third party. Let's say your name is Anne. In conversation you might say you left your car in for servicing and when you went back to collect it the mechanic said, "Anne, there's a problem with..." It's allowing the person to know your name without making it obvious.

Sometimes you will be talking with someone and you can't recall their name. Another friend comes over and you can't remember his name either. Good manners dictate you should introduce them to each other. But how? Simply say, "Why don't you introduce yourselves to each other!"

To finish off this section here's a true story: Some years back (before television) after a concert, the conductor Sir John Barbirolli was walking across the foyer of The Midland Hotel in Manchester when he saw a young woman he recognized as having met at a function. He couldn't recall her name but knew she was important. He went over and made polite conversation. Suddenly he remembered her father was well known for something. Hoping that asking about her father would give him a clue to who she was he asked, "How is your father keeping and what's he up to these days?" Came the reply, "He's very well thank and he's still the King."

Remembering Numbers

Numbers on their own are abstract symbols. Unless there is some fairly obvious pattern, it's not easy to recall them accurately. We use a two-step process which may seem complicated and off-putting at first but in reality is quite simple, yet extraordinary in its power.

This is so handy for remembering pin numbers and bank codes as well as credit card and phone numbers. You need never forget a number again.

To make the numbers memorable, each digit is represented by a sound and these sounds are represented by letters of the alphabet.

1 is always T or D, two similar sounds. D is a harder sound than T. Say each of them aloud and note the position of your tongue in relation to your teeth. The letters T and D are each made with one downstroke. That's the memory hook – one downstroke.

2 is the letter n. The N sound will always be 2. There are two downstrokes in the lowercase 'n'.

3 is the letter m. Three downstrokes or think of the 3M company. Turn the letter M sideways and it looks like 3.

4 is the letter R. And R is the last letter in fouR.

5 is L Hold up your left hand, palm away from you, with the four fingers together and the thumb outstretched. The four fingers and thumb form and *L*.

6 is the J sound which also covers CH as in chair, SH as in Shoot and the soft G sound as in gentle. J is like a mirror image of 6. Remember, it's only the sound we're interested in. The J, CH, SH and soft G sounds all come from the same place in your mouth.

7 is the K sound which includes hard C as in Crime and hard G as in Grime. K is like two 7s joined sideways.

8 is F or V or PH. The number *8* and the written *f* each contain two loops. Or what about a V-8 engine?

9 is the P or B sound. Your lips explode when you say either letter. 9 is a mirror image of P.

0 is the S sound. It includes the soft Z as in zero and the soft C as in cent

You may look at that and think you'd never learn that. But go over it with me for a minute. Look at each number and its sound. There is a memory hook for each. Go over the list twice. Visualise the memory hooks and you will have each letter and number matched up.

Did you notice that the letters used are all consonants? The vowels don't count but they will have a use in a minute. The phonetic alphabet is a two-step process. Step one is turning the numbers into sounds. But now we have to remember the sounds in the right order. And for that we use something with which we're all familiar - words.

The next step is to turn the letters into words.

Let's say your PIN number is 9271

9 is P or B

2 is N

7 is the K sound

1 is T or D.

Now to form a word using those letters B N K D. Now we use the vowels to form the consonants into words and the result is BaNKeD. In recalling the word and translating the letters back into numbers, all vowels are ignored. It is the phonetic sound of the consonant that matters.

The word CRYPT gives us C R P T translating to 7491

LITTLE gives 818. Even though there are two Ts, both are pronounced as one. It is the phonetic sound that counts.

SCENT is pronounced as CENT or SENT. It would be 021, not 0021

Let's say you want to remember the first six digits of pi. Pi is the ratio of the circumference of a circle to its diameter. And the number to remember is 3.14159.

Translated into letters 3.14159 is M T (or D) R T (or D) L P (or B). This gives us MeTeReD LiP.

Frequently the sounds will make obvious words like 235 gives us NML which becomes eNaMeL. Sometimes the sounds will take a little thought and imagination, so don't give up if your first few attempts seem difficult. You may come up with a long word or a sequence of shorter words.

While that is the very best method for recalling numbers, you might also like this method where the digits are represented by the amount of letters in a word. A one letter word represents the numeral 1, a five lettered word represents the numeral 5.

The first seven digits of pi 3.141592 would be "How I wish I could calculate pi"

Remembering Items In and Out of Order

This is an excellent system for remembering any sixteen items you might want to remember. And you can use it as a demonstration of your memory powers on your friends. Let me show you how to do it like that.

Get a pad of paper and down the left hand side write the numbers from 1 to 16. A friend (or audience member) is invited to write down the items that will be called out by members of the group. The items are to be solid objects – not abstract words and can be anything.

The first audience member calls out a number between one and sixteen as well as the item. Let's say they call out "6" and "a loaf of bread".

The helper writes 'Loaf of Bread' beside the number 6.

Next someone else calls out one of the unused numbers and another item…

"3 – a car tire".

Car tire is written beside the number 3.

And so on until there's an item beside each of the ten numbers on the list.

You proceed to go through the list from 1 to 16. Then you ask someone to call out any number and you give them the item at that number. Then they call out the item and you give its corresponding number. Finally you recite the list backwards.

This may sound like an amazing demonstration and to an audience, it is. Like all the other memory systems, it is simple and you will have no bother learning it. Just follow along with me.

Each of the numbers from 1 to 16 has a rhyming word or memory hook that goes with it, making it so easy to remember.

One	Gun
Two	Shoe
Three	Tree
Four	Door
Five	Hive (or dive)
Six	Sticks (or bricks)
Seven	Heaven
Eight	Gate
Nine	Wine (a bottle of wine)
Ten	Hen
Eleven	Spaghetti (2 long strands)
Twelve	Clock (the hands are stuck at 12)
Thirteen	Ladder (Unlucky to walk under)

Fourteen	Lightning (Lightning in the shape of 14)
Fifteen	Elevator (Going to the 15th floor)
Sixteen	Lips (Sweet Sixteen and never been kissed)

Here's how I would associate the loaf of bread with any of the numbers called:

For Gun, picture a giant water pistol (shooting loaves of bread off a wall with powerful jets of water).

For Shoe, picture the house of the old woman who lived in a shoe, or a giant multi-colored clown's shoe. (The shoe is stomping the giant loaf of bread flat).

For Tree, a big tree in full blossom with healthy green leaves (loaves of bread growing on the tree).

Four – Door see your front door brightly painted, perhaps your doorbell isn't wired properly and the current is live, so anything that touches the doorbell gets a big shock. (The loaf is the door knocker, or sparks are flying from it as it touches the doorbell).

Five – see a swarm of bees around a hive or a big blue and white diving board. (Bees airlifting the loaf into the hive).

Six – see bunches of sticks ready for a bonfire and the bonfire toasting slices of bread and the slices jumping up as if from a toaster.

Seven – Angels floating on clouds having a noisy party throwing loaves of bread at each other.

Eight – A bright yellow gate at the end of your garden. (The gate is made of iron bars and speared on the top of these are loaves of bread).

Nine – I picture the line around a football field. You can also see a big bottle of red wine. (The football players are kicking around a giant loaf of bread or the fans are throwing loaves of bread at the players).

Ten – see a large clucking hen about to lay an egg. (She's laying an enormous loaf of bread and having great difficulty doing so).

Eleven – See two large strands of spaghetti. (The spaghetti strands are slurping up the loaf of bread – or strangling it!)

Twelve – The clock with its hands stuck at twelve. (See giant loaves of bread impaled on the hands of the clock, or different sized loaves stuck where the numbers should be).

Thirteen – A ladder. (See someone walking under a ladder and loaves and loaves of bread falling on them.

Fourteen – Visualize lightning forming the shape of 14. (See the lightning strike the bread, burning it to a cinder).

Fifteen – Elevator, 15th Floor. (See loaves of bread going up and down the elevator shaft, or the elevator doors opening and hundreds of loaves of bread tumbling out).

Sixteen – Lips. Sweet sixteen and never been kissed. (Ravenous giant lips eating the bread, or big lips kissing the bread).

When given a choice of images like 'hive' or 'dive' for 5 pick, just one of them and always use it. Otherwise you will be confused during performance – you'll lose a second trying to figure out whether your mental picture is a beehive or a diving board. I always use the beehive.

When the number is called out, say 6, the bunch of sticks around the blazing bonfire immediately pops into my mind. Then I picture the loaf of bread (or whatever the item is) on the bonfire. I would see the bread being toasted and as it's done the slices shoot up in the air as though coming from a toaster. The slices of bread are shooting up all over the place. The sillier and more exaggerated the picture, the quicker and easier it will be for you to recall it.

Then go on to another number say 7 and a banjo. As soon as 7 is called I instantly have the picture of the floating angels. I now picture them all dancing around playing banjos – not like respectable angels but like country and western angels. The sillier the better.

And so on down through the list until all sixteen are filled in.

Once it's filled in call out, the list of items from 1 thru 16, making sure you have a full visual image of each item linked to its respective number. If there's any hesitation about any link, reinforce it in your mind with a stronger image.

Having done that invite anyone to call out any number. Instantly you know the item at that number. You don't even have to think. The image will be there.

After a few numbers are called out, and you've responded with the relevant items, invite the audience to call out the item and you give the number. If someone calls the 'loaf of bread' you will instantly see the slices flying out of the bonfire which is fuelled by the sticks – number 6.

After doing that a few times recite the list backwards. Just as easy.

Now here's what is absolutely vital about learning this, whether you simply use it for whatever you want to remember or as a demonstration for your friends. When someone calls out a number say, 2 and an item say a car, you must make the link between the two extremely vivid in your mind. If you simply think "2 – shoe – car, ok a car with shoes for tires", you will forget it.

The mental images you make must be EXAGGERATED. Don't just picture a car, visualise a GIANT car, or thousands of cars. The key word for 2 is shoe. You want to picture say, the old woman's shoe on top of a car with all the children looking out the windows of the shoe as the car is being driven away. When someone calls 2, the image of the shoe will instantly come to mind, and you will see it on top of the car, whizzing down the highway.

The images must use ACTION. Think of cartoon films like "Who Framed Roger Rabbit or any of the Tom & Jerry or Road Runner episodes. Characters are always banging, crashing and smashing into each other. They get squished, squashed, stretched, implode and explode. Use plenty of action in your mental images.

Cartoons are also full of vivid COLOR. Use vivid colors.

Exaggeration, action and color are the glue that lock in the mental images you visualize.

You may not believe how simple and how powerful this technique is. You may not even believe you can recall sixteen items so easily. At the start build your confidence by trying it with ten items first. Then progress to sixteen. It is no more difficult with the extra six numbers. You will have fun with this!

As we finish let's just recap the basic principles of mnemonics.

Step One: Observe. Paying attention is vital and will many times reveal an instant memory hook.

Step Two: Association. If no memory hook springs to mind, look a little deeper and make one up - Break it down. What does it sound like? What about using an acronym or acrostic? What kind of mental image can I use?

Step Three: The result – you remember.

Have you noticed the three steps Observe, Associate and Remember, themselves form an acronym? OAR. Good Luck!

References

Cleary, Thomas (1997) *The Book of Five Rings.*
Barnes and Noble Books.

Cohen, Herb (1980). *You Can Negotiate Anything.*
Bantam Books.

Daniel, Clifton (editor) (1995).
Chronicles of the 20th Century.
Dorling Kindersley Publishing, Inc.

Fear, Richard A., Chirm, Robert J. (1990).
The Evaluation Interview.
McGraw-Hill Publishing Company.

Fisher, Sharon (1997). *The Manager's Guide to Performance Management.*
HRD Press.

Karass, Chester L. (1974).
Give and Take.
New York: Thomas Y Crowell Publishers.

Krause, Donald G. (1998).
The Book of Five Rings for Executives.
Nicholas Brealey Publishing

Mackay, Harvey, (1990)
Beware The Naked Man Who Offers You His Shirt
New York: William Morrow and Company, Inc.

Mackay, Harvey, (1997)
Dig Your Well Before You're Thirsty.
A Currency Book Published by Doubleday.

Mager, Robert and Pipe, Peter (1970).
Analyzing Performance Problems.
Lake Publishing Company.

McKay, Matthew and Fanning Patrick (2000).
Self Esteem.
New York: MJK Books

McNally, David and Speak, Karl D. (2002).
Be Your Own Brand; a breakthrough formula for standing out from a crowd.
Berrett-Koehler Publishers Inc.

McWilliams, Peter (1996).
The Life 101 Quote Book.
Prelude Press.

Paterson, Randy (2000).
The Assertiveness Workbook.
New York: MJK Books.

Stewart, Charles and Cash William B. (1974). *Interviewing Principles and Practices.*
Wm C. Brown Company Publishers.

Senge, Peter M, Kleiner Art, Roberts, Charlotte, Ross, Richard B., Smith Bryan J. (1994).
The Fifth Discipline Handbook.

New York: Published by Doubleday.
Ury, William (1991).
Getting Past No.
Bantam Books.

Vedral Joyce L. (1997).
Eat To Trim.
Warner Books.

Wagenvoord, James (1985).
Personal Style. The Man's guide to Fashion, Fitness Travel and Entertaining,
New York: Holt, Rinehart and Winston.

Zi, Nancy (1986).
The Art of Breathing.
Bantam Books.

For more information about Russell Drake which includes speaking, consulting, training, and published materials, please visit his website at: www.russelldrake.com.

Printed in the United States
By Bookmasters